High Five!

eyelevelclubs

eight sessions for a children's club

Copyright © Wendy Stanbury 2007
First published 2007
ISBN 9781844272518

Scripture Union, 207–209 Queensway, Bletchley, Milton Keynes, MK2 2EB, United Kingdom.
Email: info@scriptureunion.org.uk
Website: www.scriptureunion.org.uk
Scripture Union Australia
Locked Bag 2, Central Coast Business Centre, NSW 2252, Australia
Website: www.scriptureunion.org.au
Scripture Union USA
PO Box 987, Valley Forge, PA 19482
Website: www.scriptureunion.org

Scripture quotations are from the Contemporary English Version © American Bible Society 1991, 1992, 1995, Anglicisations © British and Foreign Bible Society 1997, or from the Good News Bible © American Bible Society 1992, both published in the UK by HarperCollinsPublishers. Used by permission. Or New International Version © International Bible Society, Anglicisations © 2001, used by permission of Hodder and Stoughton Limited.

British Library Cataloguing-in-Publication Data.
A catalogue record of this book is available from the British Library.

Printed and bound by Henry Ling
Cover illustration by Brent Clark
Internal illustrations by Brent Clark
Cover and internal template design by Kevin Wade of kwgraphicdesign
Internal layout by Richard Jefferson

Scripture Union is an international Christian charity, working with churches in more than 130 countries, providing resources to bring the good news of Jesus Christ to children, young people and families and to encourage them to develop spiritually through the Bible and prayer.

As well as our network of volunteers, staff and associates who run holidays, church-based events and school Christian groups, we produce a wide range of publications and support those who use our resources through training programmes.

High Five is an *eye level* club programme, part of eye level, Scripture Union's project to catch up with children and young people who have yet to catch sight of Jesus.

For details of other *eye level* club resources and additional **High Five** material visit: www.scriptureunion.org.uk/eyelevel.

Contents Page

Starting out

Sessions

Starting out

Aims of High Five

Children need to know that Jesus loves them so much that he died for them. What's more, he longs for them to be his friend. Such a relationship makes all the difference to how a child understands life, develops as a person and develops as a member of their community. This is the BEST good news that we can ever share.

However, the majority of children know nothing about Jesus and have had little to do with his followers. But God has commissioned his followers to welcome children and to share his love with them and tell them his story. That's what **High Five**, the latest title in the *eye level* programme, is all about.

The aims are:

• To welcome children into a regular club situation so that they can experience God's love in a community of Jesus' followers.

• To share the stories of the Bible, in particular those in Mark, where Jesus touched the lives of those around him.

• To challenge children to make a further step of commitment to Jesus.

• To build relationships with the family members of children in the club.

• To follow up from *Wastewatchers*, a five-day environmental holiday club programme, although **High Five** could be used independently. The material could be used for the first eight sessions of a new children's club or could provide a term's programme teaching for a well-established group.

• To challenge children to think and care for others in the world around them.

	Session aims
Session 1 Reaching hands	**Bible story:** Jesus heals a man Mark 1:40–45 **Aim:** To understand that Jesus' hands reached out to others, crossing social boundaries to help a man with leprosy. **Social justice theme:** This session we will explore the differences and similarities between people across the world.
Session 2 Caring hands	**Bible story:** Jesus heals a man who was deaf and could hardly talk Mark 7:31–37 **Aim:** To recognise the way in which Jesus' hands cared for those who would have been unable to help themselves. **Social justice theme:** This session we will start to look at Fairtrade food.
Session 3 Sharing hands	**Bible story:** Jesus feeds 4,000 Mark 8:1–10 **Aim:** To understand how Jesus met the needs of people by feeding a huge group of his listeners. With his hands he shared out the food. **Social justice theme:** This session we will continue looking at Fairtrade food.
Session 4 Welcoming hands	**Bible story:** Who is the greatest? Mark 9:33–37 **Aim:** To understand that Jesus welcomed people with outstretched hands (maybe not always literally), however insignificant or important they were. **Social justice theme:** This session we will be thinking about children without choices.
Session 5 Giving hands	**Bible story:** A rich man, and a widow's offering Mark 10:17–31; Mark 12:41–44 **Aim:** To understand that Jesus expects us to give, but it is our attitude in giving that counts, not really how *much* we give. Jesus came ultimately to give his own life! **Social justice theme:** This session we will continue to think about children without choices.
Session 6 Loving hands	**Bible story:** The request of James and John, and the most important commandment: to love God and others Mark 10:32–45; Mark 12:28–34 **Aim:** To recognise that loving God and loving others as much as ourselves are the two most important commandments, which James and John had not really grasped. (They thought they would be accepted by Jesus by right!) **Social justice theme:** This session we look at water conservation, giving examples of the way in which we can help others in our world.
Session 7 Hurting hands	**Bible story:** Jesus is nailed to a cross Mark 14:43–52; Mark 15:24–28,33–37 **Aim:** To understand that throughout his life Jesus changed people's lives. To understand that Jesus loves us so much that he died on the cross with nails hammered through his hands (or wrists). **Social justice theme:** Change one thing! This session we're looking at the 'Change One Thing' campaign.
Session 8 Strong hands	**Bible story:** Jesus is alive! Mark 16:1–7 **Aim:** To know that Jesus died on the cross for each one of us, but then rose from the dead. His hands are indeed strong hands. **Social justice theme:** We will be reviewing all the **High Five** themes.

How the programme works

Each session is divided into five parts counting down from five to one. The sections are:
Countdown 5: Hands up for fun and games
Countdown 4: Open the Bible
Countdown 3: Keep those hands busy
Countdown 2: Joining hands around the world
Countdown 1: Hands to praise and hands to pray

If you work to the suggested timings of each *Countdown*, as shown below, you will have a programme that takes about an hour and a half. To extend your programme, take extra time on the craft activities and, at the same time, chat with your group about the things they have learnt in the rest of the session. *Countdown 4* is designed so that you do all of the activities but for the rest of the *Countdowns* you will need to choose those that are most suitable for your group as you won't have time to do everything. (Timings are also given for each activity.) Be aware of the attention span of your children, their backgrounds and past experiences of being part of a church community when making your selections.

An activity for a small group is marked
An activity for older children is marked

Countdown 5: Hands up for fun and games
(20 minutes)

This is a selection of fun activities involving movement, games, and action whilst introducing the session's aim and story. This is a good way for everyone to enjoy being together whilst letting off steam at the beginning of the session. Vary your choice of activities according to the mood of the children as they arrive, the type of venue you have, the number of helpers and the time available.

Make sure that this *Countdown* has pace so that you have time for the other sessions and so children don't get bored.

Countdown 4: Open the Bible
(20–30 minutes)

This *Countdown* is the main teaching session, based on the Bible story being read out in a variety of ways followed by group discussions and activities. It is intended that you complete all of the activities rather than making a selection. Bible reading is deliberately central to this programme. That is why the key Bible passages are included (see pages 50–53) so that you can put them on an OHP acetate or reproduce them in some way. The Bible will be part of a child's life long after you have left and the club has ended, so be imaginative in how you use it! Your enthusiasm for God's Word will be infectious. Suggestions are given on ways of reading the Bible passage in an imaginative way, such as using a story bag or props, or by encouraging the children to read out parts, or act out the emotions of the characters involved.

All the Bible passages come from Mark's Gospel. The Bible verses have been reproduced from the Contemporary English Version and used with permission. This version is especially good for reading out loud. But whatever version of the Bible you use, make sure it is child-friendly and doesn't look old or out of date.

In sessions 4 and 6 there are Bible verses for the children to learn and remember. These can be taught in one session and then used and recapped in the following one. Feel free to teach the verse earlier or later in your session – wherever you feel is most appropriate for your group.

Countdown 3: Keep those hands busy
(20 minutes)

This *Countdown* provides a choice of craft activities to continue the theme of the session. It is a good opportunity to get alongside the children and to continue talking about the Bible passage or the theme for the day and for them to ask you any questions they may have. Often the craft items that are made are used in *Countdown 1* which may give the children more incentive to make something they are proud of!

Countdown 2: Joining hands around the world
(10 minutes)

In this *Countdown* children are encouraged to think about the wider world and, in particular, issues related to social justice. In most cases the social justice issue is closely linked to the theme of the session. So, for example, in session 3, children will explore how Jesus met the needs of the people by feeding a huge crowd, and the social justice issue looks at Fairtrade food.

Countdown 1: Hands to praise and hands to pray

(10 minutes)

This *Countdown* includes ideas to help the children respond through creative prayer, in a variety of ways. Even if you find you are often short of time near the end of your club, do include a prayer idea, at least sometimes.

Have you ever tried singing in your children's club? There are lots of excellent tracks on children's praise and worship CDs which you can sing along with even if you don't have a musician. Songs can be included to start your session off or at the end. Look out for songs which involve actions but be sure to include some quieter, reflective songs as well as more lively ones. Here are a few suggestions about God's love, compassion, acceptance and power, which are some of the themes of **High Five**. Be careful, though, to ensure that you are not putting words in the children's mouths which they cannot personally mean.

'All the time!' (*RU*)
'Anyone can come to God' (*RU*)
'Children of the world' (*LFE*)
'Follow me' (*BBS*)
'For God so loved the world' (*KS464*)
'God made you and me' (*LFE*)
'He's got the whole world' (*JP78*)
'Jesus never' (*KS602*)
'Jesus went out of his way' (*KS610*)
'Love the Lord' (*BBS*)
'Streetwise' (*LFE*)
'Taller than the mountains' (*RU*)
'Twisting back in time' (*LFE*)
'Who took fish and bread?' (*JP286*)

BBS (SU *Bitesize Bible Songs* CD)
JP (*Junior Praise*)
KS (*Kidsource*)
LFE (SU *Light for Everyone* CD)
RU (SU *Reach Up!* CD)

Other resources

Use these books as a final gift to each child who has been in the club, or use throughout the club:

Bible Codecrakers: Jesus
£3.99 64pp
The story of Jesus brought to life for 8 to 11s using Bible text, retold story and challenging puzzles.

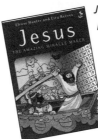

Jesus – the amazing miracle maker
£1.99 32pp
Explore the life of Jesus through puzzles, codes, mazes, wordsearches and more! For 5 to 7s.

(Prices correct at the time of going to print.)

All of these are available from good local Christian bookshops or from SU Mail Order: Scripture Union Mail Order, PO Box 5148, Milton Keynes MLO, MK2 2YX
Tel: 0845 07 06 006 Fax: 01908 856020
Web: www.scriptureunion.org.uk

Storytelling

Telling the story of how Jesus reached out to touch people's lives is an essential feature of **High Five**. Each week children will find out a bit more about who Jesus is and how he can touch our lives. However, many people feel that they are not gifted in storytelling and prefer to watch a video or read the story from a children's book of Bible stories. The aim of this page is to help you rekindle what might be a dying art form.

✺ Know the facts

Often we think that we know a Bible story – after all, we heard it when we were children! Don't simply rely on your memory – read the biblical text through before you look in a children's Bible.

As you read you might find it helpful to jot down the order of events, key facts, key people and content of speeches. If the story contains difficult words or unfamiliar concepts think about how these can be simplified or explained as part of the story.

✺ Different story methods

Most children learn through seeing and doing rather than by hearing alone. Involving different learning styles as you tell a story can greatly help a child's concentration and retention of the facts.
• If you can draw well or have access to picture books you could display illustrations. (Why not use the SU publication *How to cheat at Visual Aids* which contains pictures of Bible characters and scenes?)
• If the story has some repeated key words, ask the children to listen out for them and then respond with actions, or play a team game and every time a particular word is mentioned the children race round their team and back to their place.
• Story bags are increasingly popular in school and you could make one of these yourself and include different items that feature in the story.
• If there are a lot of nouns then think about playing a drawing game before you tell the story or play 'hangman' as you go through.

• Another fun way is to read the story straight from the Bible and then reread it with some mistakes for the children to spot.
• Children love acting and miming – particularly if everyone can be involved in a crowd scene. Alternatively, ask leaders to act or be interviewed as if they had been with Jesus.
• If you are more creative then make some simple puppets by dressing wooden spoons or sticking faces to cardboard cones.

You will probably find that different leaders enjoy different methods so vary what you do through the series to give the children different learning experiences.

✺ Start and finish well

Even if you have wonderful pictures or exciting props and puppets you will still have to relate the story in your own words. If your group has been involved in energetic games or the children are still sticky from craft then keeping their attention is important. Start with confidence, having planned your first sentence in advance so that it grabs their imagination and finds them eager to discover what happens.

The final sentence is important too – you don't want the story simply to fade away. Perhaps this sentence could sum up your main teaching point.

✺ Telling the story

As you tell the story, use your face and voice to convey different feelings such as being happy, sad, proud, angry, surprised or worried. Try to change your pitch and tone for characters or different situations they find themselves in.

If someone is running or excited then speak more quickly, or if they are pondering something then speak more slowly. As you reach the climax of the story, or just before something exciting happens, pause and then speak in a quieter voice. Move around your stage area as the story changes venue and use your body and hands to mime actions such as stretching out your hand to the man with leprosy or breaking the bread and handing it around at the feeding of the 4,000.

✿ Use your voice

Make sure you speak naturally and sound interested in the story yourself – if you have to read it then know the script well enough to add expression.

And finally – there is nothing that can take the place of practice, practice and even more practice!

✿ Storytelling ideas

For pictures to use in storytelling see page 57

Have a look at the different storytelling methods used in this material:
1 Children read out parts (session 1)
2 Leader reads the passage and the children listen out for specific things (session 2)
3 Children read parts and use props (session 3)
4 Children act out parts (session 4)
5 Leader uses pictures then children act out what happened next (session 5)
6 Leader reads as play, children act out parts (session 6)
7 Children imagine the scene with eyes shut as story is read out (session 7)
8 Leader takes items out of story bag (session 8)

Getting to know you

✹ Building relationships

The children you'll meet at **High Five** live in a fast-moving, sophisticated, technology-orientated world, dominated by screens. There is so much 'stuff' demanding their attention. Rather than trying to compete with that sort of environment, offer them what they are often missing elsewhere – real communication. Concentrate on the unique opportunity you have to build relationships, listen to them, talk with them, and give them time as you show them God's love in action. That way they will get to know you, each other and Jesus on their **High Five** adventure, and have a great time too!

✹ Top tips for sharing Jesus with children

• **Build strong friendships**. Be genuinely interested in their lives, homes, interests, what happens at school. These friendships will be bridges across which Jesus can walk! Ensure that these children know that you appreciate and respect them.

• **Be informed** about what is happening at school and home – it's useful to be in the know about sports days, class excursions or family events, and these may explain why the children are excited or tired, or both!

• **Get to know the children's families**. Understand their home lives, and help their parents (or whoever is responsible for their care) know what they are learning. Children can never be divorced from their home backgrounds. Avoid talking about Mum and Dad. It's best to refer to Mum *or* Dad or even, 'whoever looks after you at home'.

• **Remember birthdays**, or ask someone else to take on the responsibility of noting dates and preparing cards, perhaps for the other children to sign.

• **Do as you say!** The children need to see you model what you teach them. Your friendship with Jesus matters. How else will the children see what it means in practice to be in a relationship with him?

• **Encourage everyone to join in**, adults and children alike. Create a 'we're in this together' feel to the sessions, rather than 'them and us'. Avoid organising activities that adults stand and watch. Relax, have fun and learn with the children – *'Aim to give children the best hour of their week!'* Dave Connelly, Frontline Church.

• **Mind your language!** Avoid jargon words (eg sin, grace or churchy words) and explain what you mean by things like prayer.

• **Use illustrations from everyday life** to explain concepts. Jesus taught complex truths in simple ways eg 'You can't see wind, but you can see the effects that it has; it's the same with the Holy Spirit'. You will need to think about this before the club begins.

• **Grow the children's confidence with the Bible** and explain how to read it. Why don't we often start at page 1? How do we use the Contents page? (Younger children find this very hard.) What are the differences between chapters and verses, or the Old and New Testaments? How do you explain that the Bible is one big story – God's story – in different bits? Find out more about the Bible in *The Story of the Book* (see page 63).

• **Talk about Jesus**, rather than God, where possible. The Gospels give us clear pictures of what he is like and these are far easier to grasp than the idea of God being 'up there' but invisible. Children have some very woolly ideas about God, but there is less room for manoeuvre when it comes to Jesus! You will have plenty of opportunities to talk about Jesus as **High Five** is centred round Jesus' life and resurrection.

• **Apply the Bible teaching appropriately**: 'If Jesus arrived in your town, like he arrived in Jerusalem, what do you think he would say and do? How do you think people would welcome him?' Help them see that Jesus is alive today (even though we can't see him) and is relevant to their lives.

• **Allow children to make responses** that are appropriate for them, their understanding and their backgrounds. Don't rush straight in with, 'Do you want to follow Jesus?' That should be a decision that lasts for life, and they need to recognise what it entails. For many children, there are a number of commitments as their understanding grows.

• **Have fun together!** The children need to catch something of the 'life in all its fullness' that Jesus spoke about.

Working with small groups

✳ Practicalities

- Children are all different. Respect their differences.
- Make sure any child with a special need is catered for.
- Make sure children know they can come to you with any questions.
- Make sure that children are comfortable. Cold, hard floors do not encourage positive discussion. Cushions, mats or comfortable chairs can make all the difference. Sometimes, everyone lying on their tummies in a star shape can create a fantastic atmosphere – their teacher at school is unlikely to do this!
- Keep good eye contact with every child.
- In the group, watch out for children who are on the edge.
- Don't talk down to children – talk *with* them. This means getting to their level, physically and verbally.
- Don't always rush to fill silences while children are thinking of responses.
- Validate all responses, either by a further question or ask others what they think, especially if you don't agree with the initial comment or answer.
- If lots of children want to talk, pass an object round – only the child holding the object can speak.
- Encourage children to listen to each other (something they might find quite difficult).
- Be prepared to admit that you don't know the answer to a question, but say that you'll find out the answer, if appropriate.

✳ Asking questions

There are plenty of opportunities in **High Five** for asking the children questions about the Bible passage and encouraging their thinking about God. A discussion is most appropriate when the children are in small groups as they don't need to wait as long for an opportunity to speak.

Ever thought about the kinds of questions you ask people? The same question can be asked in many different ways, and force the person being asked the question to give certain kinds of answers.

?? Rhetorical

If you ask, 'Isn't it great to have ice cream?' it is a **rhetorical question**, implying the expected answer. It brings out the right answer for the benefit of others.

?? Closed

If you ask, 'Do you like coming to **High Five**?' it is a **closed question**, mainly allowing for 'Yes' or 'No'. It encourages contributions and assesses what the children think.

?? Factual

If you ask, 'What food did Jesus give the crowd of people?' it is a **factual question**, requiring basic information. It encourages contributions and establishes the facts.

?? Open

If you ask, 'Why did Jesus' disciples argue about who was the greatest?' it is an **open question**, allowing broad expression. It encourages discussion and indicates what the children think.

?? Experience

If you ask, 'Have you ever been in a situation where you have found it hard to give – like the rich young ruler?' it is an **experience question**, for sharing views or feelings. It encourages discussion and helps children to apply the teaching personally.

?? Leading

If you ask, 'What have you learnt at **High Five**, Anna?' it is a **leading question** aimed at getting a specific answer from someone. It indicates learning and understanding and encourages contributions.

Think about when you might use these types of questions in your group. Go through each question with your team and decide when it is appropriate and when it is inappropriate to use certain kinds of questions.

Helping children respond

✳ Being Jesus' friend

High Five introduces children to Jesus. The children will find out about the awesome God who loves and cares for us, and who came to rescue us and help us to be his friends. They will see that we should always thank him, and obey him. They will also learn that Jesus can forgive us for all the wrong we ever do. This may prompt the children to want to know Jesus personally. Be ready to help them.

• They rarely need long explanations, just simple answers to questions.
• Talk to them in a place where you can be seen by others.
• Never put pressure on children to respond in a particular way, just help them take one step closer to Jesus when they are ready. We don't want them to respond just to please us!
• Remember, many children make a commitment to Jesus, followed by further commitments as they mature and their understanding grows.
• Many children just need a bit of help to say what they want to say to God. Here is a suggested prayer they could use to make a commitment to Jesus:

Jesus, I want to be your friend.
Thank you that you love me.
Thank you for living in the world and dying on a cross for me.
I'm sorry for all the wrong things I have done.
Please forgive me and let me be your friend.
Please let the Holy Spirit help me be like you.
Amen.

Reassure them that God hears us when we talk with him and has promised to forgive us and help us be his friends.

✳ What next?

Children need help to stick with Jesus, especially if their parents don't believe.
• Assure them that God wants them to talk with him, whatever they want to say. Give them some prayer ideas.
• Encourage them to keep coming to Christian activities, not necessarily on Sundays – their 'church' might be the midweek club or a school lunchtime club.

• Reading the Bible will be easier with something like *Snapshots* – but you need to support them if they are to keep it up. It may be appropriate to give them a Bible as well. Make sure that this is not seen as a reward for becoming a Christian.
• Keep praying and maintain your relationship with them wherever possible.

✳ Some booklets from Scripture Union that may help

Friends with Jesus
A booklet explaining what it means to make a commitment to follow Jesus for 8s and under.
978 1 84427 141 2 (single) £0.99
978 1 84427 144 3 (pack of 20) £15.00

Me+Jesus
A booklet explaining what it means to make a commitment to follow Jesus for 8 to 10s.
978 1 84427 142 9 (single) £0.99
978 1 84427 145 0 (pack of 20) £15.00

Jesus=friendship forever
A booklet explaining what it means to make a commitment to follow Jesus for 10 to 12s.
978 1 84427 143 6 (single) £0.99
978 1 84427 146 7 (pack of 20) £15.00

What Jesus did
D Abrahall
A book exploring Jesus, ideal for those with special needs.
978 1 84427 005 7 (single) £2.00
978 1 84427 006 4 (pack of 5 with teachers' guide) £8.00

Snapshots
Bible reading for 8 to 11s
£3.00 single copy
UK £11.00 annual subscription
£15.00 packs of 6
£0.99 4–week challenge (978 1 84427 086 6)

(*Prices are correct at the time of going to press.*)
For a simple commitment card, visit the *eye level* website: www.scriptureunion.org.uk/eyelevel

Sharing your faith

So many people put their trust in Jesus because they have heard how important he is to someone else. You have a great opportunity to share with the children what Jesus means to different people, and also to show by the way you live your own life that Jesus really is alive! Here are some pointers to bear in mind when you're talking with children about what Jesus means to you:

• Make sure you don't use Christian jargon or concepts that just don't make sense – 'Inviting Jesus into your heart' might suggest to some children that Jesus is only welcome in a bit of them. The idea of a person you can't see living inside your body can be a bit spooky!

• Remember you are talking to children whose experience of life is not as broad as an adult's, so their uncertainties and questions are different. Address their issues by referring to experiences which are relevant to them. This is not necessarily just what it was like for you when you were a child! But, for example, the emotions you experienced when you recently changed job may be very similar to those of a child changing school. God was with you then, so he can be with a child.

• Speak about Jesus as someone you know and are enthusiastic about.

• Make reference to what the Bible says in a way that makes a child want to read the Bible for themselves – sound enthusiastic about what God has said to us. Hold the Bible with respect and read it with interest. Tell a Bible story briefly to explain a point.

• Be brief and speak with simple sentences, using appropriate language.

• Be honest, talking about the good and the bad times. God doesn't always give answers straightaway, or the answers we want.

• It is important to talk about what Jesus means to us now and not when we first came to know him dozens of years ago.

If you are involved in upfront presentation, there are some other points to consider:

• An interview process is less intense and invites the children to engage with what the interviewee is saying.

• Include questions or information about subjects such as favourite colours, food, team, job, hopes, worst moments, as well as a favourite Bible character or story. Think what a child is curious about. 'Normal' information communicates that being a Christian is all about Jesus being with us all the time, being normal!

• Not everyone's experience will be appropriate, however dramatic it might be! Long and complicated stories will lose children. A wide age range of children will also determine what is suitable.

• Use someone's story which is relevant to the theme of the day.

• Over the weeks, choose a variety of people with different experiences to share what Jesus means to them.

• It would be worth the team hearing what is going to be said in advance, if someone's experience is going to raise questions that may be a challenge to answer.

• Whether you're speaking in front of the whole club, or one child, you should be ready to tell your story. Think beforehand about what you are going to say, just as you would practise music or drama. It isn't a speech but there is no excuse for rambling.

Practical considerations

It is important to think about child protection when running your club. If your midweek club has already been in existence for some time, you have probably made all the necessary arrangements. However, if you are just starting up a midweek club, there is child protection advice on the Scripture Union website. For advice specific to running a holiday club, see the child protection section in *Wastewatchers*.

What to do after High Five

⚙ Step one – time to think

Hopefully **High Five** has made you think about how you run activities and reach out to children in your community. Before the end of the **High Five** series, plan a review with anyone who helped. Be as honest as you can and dream dreams!
• What did the children enjoy about **High Five**?
• What was different compared to your previous activities for children?
• Were there more small group activities? How did they work?
• Was there more Bible input than before?
• What worked really well or didn't work?
• What did the leaders enjoy?
• What did you discover about each other's gifts for working with children? Was there an unknown storyteller or someone especially good at welcoming children?

Write down the most important answers. Talk about what you should do next.

⚙ Step two – moving on

Don't be afraid to develop what you provide for children. If **High Five** encouraged you to run a midweek or Saturday club for the first time and it worked, plan to carry on. You may need extra help, especially if some people can't commit themselves weekly. Perhaps you could continue your club next term or maybe a monthly Saturday/Sunday special, using another Scripture Union programme.

Discuss how you might contact new children. What are your links with the local school(s) or neighbourhood groups? Could you publicise your group through the local paper or library? How could the children who already come be encouraged to bring their friends? Just how many more children can you cope with?

⚙ Step three – building on High Five

One of the aims of **High Five** is to bring children who don't usually have much contact with a Christian community into a Christian activity. If this worked for you, build on the final **High Five** session and get to know the children's families by running a parents' special event. Family games work well, either games to play within families or families competing against one another. Any family activity that offers food will be popular! Alternatively, some churches have explored parenting groups. In one place a church football team has developed from fathers of children who started coming to a church children's club. Be imaginative and find out what other churches have done in your area. Maybe you could do something together.

Whatever you do, try to maintain contact with children, to sustain and grow your relationships. You may wish to visit them at home, to deliver a birthday card or to let parents know the starting date for next term or to invite families to a family event or special service such as a carol service. If you do home visits make sure parents are happy for you to come and contact them to arrange a time for your visit.

⚙ Other programmes

Streetwise, Awesome! and *Clues2Use*, eight-session programmes similar in aim and design to **High Five**, are already available. *Streetwise*, with an accompanying DVD (based on the *Luke Street* video), introduces children to the inhabitants of various houses Jesus visited, using Luke's Gospel. *Awesome!* and its accompanying DVD (based on the *Signposts* video) find signs to who Jesus is in the Gospel of John. *Clues2Use*, which follows on from the *Landlubbers* holiday club programme, is based on Luke's Gospel and uses the *Jesus Quest* DVD.

Look out for *Wastewatchers*, a five-day environmental holiday club programme based on Genesis 1 and 2 and John's Gospel, as children discover God's transformation in creation and in the lives of all those who follow Christ.

All of these are available from good local Christian bookshops or from SU Mail Order:
Scripture Union Mail Order, PO Box 5148, Milton Keynes MLO, MK2 2YX
Tel: 0845 07 06 006 Fax: 01908 856020
Web: www.scriptureunion.org.uk

Extra activities

The first and last few minutes of a club can be the most important! Your first conversation with a child helps to settle them, for them to be open to God. You represent Jesus: your welcome is his welcome. The end of the club may be what they remember best, so make the most of the time.

A few guidelines

• Choose the right opening question for the right day: if it's the weekend, keep school conversation to a minimum.
• Be led by the child. Don't probe where they don't want to talk.
• Allow a conversation to develop rather than just asking questions.
• Help others join in as they join the group.
• Tell the children about your day to build friendships and make it less like a grilling.

Questions about school

What was the best thing that happened? Did anything funny happen? What did you have for dinner? What's the food like at your school?

General questions

What have you seen on television/read/done recently? What are you doing this weekend? How's your football team doing? Tell me about your family/pets/what you do in your spare time.

Ideas to end the club

A routine pattern to the end may be useful:

In groups

• Chat about what they will do at home/later/during the week.
• A quick recap of the Bible teaching to help them remember/apply it.
• Pray for the week ahead.

Together

• Recap the Bible teaching and allow a moment to think about it again.
• Sing the same song each week which has become the theme song for the club.

One after-school club always concludes with a short prayer followed by a 'wind-up Amen' where everyone starts saying 'Amen' softly and ends up shouting it. One classroom teacher asked a leader of the club what it was that the children always shouted at the end! It was a good opening to share about prayer!

Time-fillers

• Turn everyone's name round and enjoy the different sounds! (Nhoj Htims, Enna Senoj)
• I Spy. For very young children play 'I spy with my colour eye', with objects of a certain colour.
• Who can… wiggle their ears, touch their nose with their tongue, recite the alphabet backwards, wiggle their eyebrows? And so on.
• Dice games: have ready-made cards with questions to be answered when the numbers are rolled. For example:
Favourites: 1 – food; 2 – pop group; 3 – team; 4 – TV programme; 5 – story; 6 – colour.
Home: 1 – family; 2 – rooms; 3 – pets; 4 – food; 5 – outside the house; 6 – favourite room.
Favourite food: 1 – sandwich; 2 – drink; 3 – breakfast; 4 – biscuits; 5 – snack; 6 – worst food.
• Simon Says.
• 'I went to the park (supermarket, football match) and I saw…' Each person recites the growing list and adds an item.
• Mime things you do at home – others must guess, eg watching TV, turning on a tap, cleaning teeth.
• Challenge the group to use their bodies to make a human sculpture of household objects, eg a chair, knife and fork, clock, bathroom.

If the children's arrival is staggered, you may want to have a general activity that they can join in as they arrive. Or you might want to have an ongoing activity, which the children can do as a group craft.

1

Session 1
Reaching hands

Mark 1:40–45
Jesus heals a man

Aim
To understand that Jesus' hands reached out to others, crossing social boundaries to help a man with leprosy.

Social justice theme
This session we will explore the differences and similarities between people across the world.

Jesus showed compassion and touched the man when others would not have gone near him. Today, people can be excluded on all sorts of grounds including appearance, race, disability and age. Children recognise that we are all the same but different. We can reach out to others in the way that Jesus did. All children will be challenged during the session to think about how Jesus' actions should shape the way we behave towards others. We may not be able to heal diseases, but we can certainly reach out to those who are left out!

Countdown 5:

Hands up for fun and games

Choose one or more of these activities (depending on time) to introduce today's theme to your group.

 Swap around
5 minutes

What you do
Stand with the children in a large circle. Explain that you are going to give a 'swap' instruction and, if it applies to them, the children should follow that. Give instructions such as, 'Swap places if you are wearing a T-shirt/wearing blue/have brown eyes.' The person who is last to change places is out. Each time, choose a different reason for swapping places. Other suggestions might be, 'Swap places if you have a brother,' or 'If you are in Year 6.' From time to time, call out, 'Everyone swap!'

After the game, discuss how we often judge people on the basis of how they look or what they have. Is this fair? What experiences do the children have where this has happened to them or people they know? How did they feel? What did they do? What could they have done? Explain that you are going to hear about someone who was left out because they had a disease.

 Islands
5 minutes

What you need
• Four or five hoops (carpet tiles or large sheets of newspaper could be used instead)
• Drum

What you do
Scatter four or five hoops around the floor. Ask the children to run around. When the drum bangs they get into the hoop (or onto the paper or tile) in groups of three. In those groups, find out three things that they have in common with each other, and one thing that is different. Repeat several times, each time getting into a different group of three. Note, this is the opposite of musical chairs which ultimately excludes all but one person!

As a whole group, share the things they have in common with each other and the differences they discovered. Were there any things that surprised them? Today, you will hear about a man who was different which meant he was left out.

 **Reach out**
5 minutes

What you need
• Drum

What you do
Organise the children into pairs. Choose who is going to be A and B. Ask the children to run around with A following B, until the drum bangs and both A and B stop. A, staying in the same stopping position, needs to reach B. If A can touch B, they get the point. If not, then B gets the point. Next time, swap around so that B needs to reach A when the drum bangs.

Jesus reached out to all people, whoever they were. Today's session is going to focus on one of those people that Jesus reached out to, whom others would have nothing to do with.

 **Sticky dots**
5 minutes

What you need
• Sticky dots of four different colours

What you do

Stick a dot on each forehead using only three colours so that the children cannot see which colour they are. Stick one dot of the fourth colour on one child's forehead (make sure you choose a confident child). Ask the children to get into groups depending on the colour on their forehead. There should be three groups of children wearing the same colour, and one child alone. How does it feel to be the one person left out? When does this kind of situation arise in everyday life – at school, at playtime, in our families?

Countdown 4:

Open the Bible

 Read the story
5 minutes

What you need

• Bibles or photocopies of page 50

What you do

Sit together in a circle. Either read the story in Mark 1:40–45 to the group or, if you have confident readers in your group, ask one child to be the narrator, one to be Jesus and another to be the man. Ask the children to listen out for why the man was always left out. How might he feel? You will need to explain that, at the time of Jesus, people were scared that they would catch skin diseases from someone if they went near them or touched them. Anyone suffering from one had to live on the edge of the community with other sufferers.

Discuss why people are excluded today. What modern day situations could be put into this story? Are there people in our neighbourhood or school who are avoided by others? Has this ever happened to someone we know? Issues of race and disability may be raised for sensitive discussion at this point. Jesus wanted to help this man, so why do the children think he might help people in our world who are left out? What does this show them about Jesus? In what ways might he want to help us?

Explore the story further using one or more of the suggestions below:

⚉2 In the hot seat
10 minutes

What you need

• Cloak, throw or headdress to dress up an adult as the healed man

What you do

Before the session, ask another leader to pretend to be the man with leprosy. In pairs, invite the children to devise two questions they would like to ask the healed man, eg 'Why did you think Jesus would be able to help you?' 'How did you feel when Jesus said he wanted to help you?' 'What did it feel like when Jesus healed you?' The children can then put their questions to the dressed-up leader who should answer in character, imagining what the healed man might have said. The leader should mention something of Jesus' compassion if possible – that he *wanted* to heal him. That would have been unheard of for the man with leprosy!

⚉3 How did they feel?
10 minutes

What you need

• Copies of page 50
• Felt-tip pens

What you do

Put the children in small groups and give each group a copy of the story and felt-tip pens. Read it through together then ask the children to take the story and think about the emotions of Jesus and the man with leprosy, and the reactions of the people who heard the man's amazing story. They then draw faces next to the relevant Bible verses, according to how the characters were feeling. Bring everyone together to share ideas and thoughts, deciding between you how all the characters would have felt. Discuss how brave the man must have been to talk to Jesus and how kind Jesus was to help him. Jesus touched him – if anyone saw it, they would have been very surprised!

A smaller group could do this together, using an enlarged copy of the verses.

World of a child

In this very short story, we encounter something of Jesus' emotions and desires. He feels sorry for the man and wants to heal him. This may speak strongly to children from a church background. They are often told that Jesus *can* help them, but here they find that Jesus *wants* to help them – quite a different prospect! For non-churched children, this may be their first encounter with Jesus' healing power and with Jesus as a person. He feels compassion for people and wants to help them!

Countdown 3:

Keep those hands busy

All the items produced during this part of the session can be used later as part of the focus on praise and prayer in *Countdown 1*. Use the time to talk about the story the children have just heard, and their reactions to it. The aim of this activity is not always to produce a finished piece of craft, but to use the time as a chance to catch up with the children's understanding of the story and what they have discovered about Jesus.

 Handprint pictures

20 minutes

What you need
- Trays of paint in a range of colours (powder paint or ready-mix paint is the best for this type of activity)
- Large sheets of paper
- Scissors
- Glue

What you do
Paint handprints and footprints in a range of colours, and then allow these to dry before cutting them out. (If you are short of time, do this as your *Countdown 5* activity. The prints should then be dry by the time you come to cut them out.) The children should make pictures with these hand and footprints, either individually or as a group eg leaves on a tree from green handprints, tree trunks from brown footprints, clouds from white or grey handprints, plants and flowers from a range of coloured prints. Once the group or individuals have decided where to place the prints, they can be stuck on the large sheet of paper. Additional fine details can then be painted on, using a brush.

As you work together, chat about the way in which so many unique parts can make a whole picture. Explore the idea that we are all the same, yet all different. But all our differences and similarities help to make the complete picture. Jesus did not exclude people on the basis of their differences, but accepted people for who they were.

 Photo frames

20 minutes

What you need
- Thin cardboard
- Photo frame template from page 54
- Glue
- Scissors
- Paint or felt-tip pens
- Collage materials

What you do
Using the template provided cut out the two pieces of the photo frame from the thin cardboard. Glue the outside edges of both pieces and stick together. The photo frame can be decorated with paints or felt-tip pens and collage materials.

The children either bring in a photo from home for the following session to put inside the photo frame or a photo could be taken this session using a digital camera, to be printed and placed in the frame. (This needs to be done in accordance with your church's policy on children and photography.)

When the frames are complete with the photo, talk about them together. Make the point about our differences and similarities. Jesus reached out to care for all people, whoever they were, even if they were rejected by others for being different in some way.

 Collage portraits

20 minutes

What you need
- Large sheets of paper
- Scissors
- Glue
- Small squares of colour cut from magazine pictures, cut out beforehand
- Mirror

What you do
Ask the children to look in a mirror and talk about what they see. What similarities are there with other members of the group? What are the differences? On a large piece of paper, the children draw just the outline of their head and shoulders. Group together the cut out magazine squares, eg squares of flesh tones in one pile, squares of brown hair colour in another. Physical features such as eyes, noses and mouths can also be cut out and grouped together. Use these squares of colour to form a collage self-portrait, asking a friend to help with the right choice of

colours. The basic hair and skin colours should be stuck on to fill the head outline.

When the whole head is covered with the right hair and skin tones, then features such as eyes, nose and mouth can be stuck on, choosing the features that most resemble their own in terms of colour and shape.

Finally, use squares of colour cut from magazines to fill in the shoulders. They could choose their favourite colour for this, or a colour that they often wear.

After the collage has been completed, talk about the finished self-portrait collage. Which collages are good likenesses? Discuss how difficult it was to find just the right colour or shape, because we are all so unique. Despite the similarities between us, we are all special and different. Remind the children of the way in which Jesus reached out to all people, whether they were similar to him or regarded as different like the man with leprosy in the story.

Countdown 2:

Joining hands around the world

In this section encourage the children to focus on the similarities between themselves and children around the world, not just the differences.

 World focus
10 minutes

What you need
- Pictures of children from around the world
- Pencils or pens
- Paper

What you do
Look at pictures of children in a variety of settings from other countries (produced by the Salvation Army International Development Department www.salvationarmy.org.uk/id). In groups of two or three, identify those things that are the same about themselves and the children in the pictures and then list the things which are different. List these in two columns on a piece of paper in their groups, or feed ideas into a whole group discussion with a leader as scribe, on a large piece of paper.

What does the story that we heard about Jesus reaching out to others tell us about how we should respond to others? Jesus has the power to heal and wants to help people and restore them to true life. How does this challenge them to help others in different parts of the world?

 Ideas factory
😊 *10 minutes*

What you need
- Pictures of children from around the world, each stuck onto a large sheet of paper. The children need to come from a variety of settings from other countries. (See Salvation Army International Development Department www.salvationarmy.org.uk/id).
- Large felt-tip pens or marker pens

What you do
In groups of two or three the children look at one picture and think of some ideas and words about that picture. They write them down adding questions they may have. They then move on to the next picture/image. Eventually, the children should work their way round all the images so that each large sheet of paper is full of the accumulated ideas and questions.

Allow time to share these ideas and discuss them as a whole group. How does the story about Jesus reaching out to others challenge us about how we should respond to others?

Countdown 1:

Hands to praise and hands to pray

If your group is used to singing songs, use this time to do so. 'Jesus never' would be an appropriate song for the theme for this session (or see page 7 for further suggestions). Otherwise, here are some other worship and prayer activities you can try out. Maybe you could introduce the idea of singing to God?

 Handprint prayers
5–10 minutes

What you need
- One of the handprints you created from *Countdown 3* for each child
- Pens or pencils

What you do
Give out the handprints, ideally giving each child their own handprint. Ask the children to look at the print and think about how Jesus can

1

help them in their lives. After a couple of minutes, ask everyone to write on their handprint what they have thought about. Round off with a prayer thanking Jesus that he cares for us all and wants to help us all, even though we are all different with different needs.

Go on to do *Activity 3* 'Prayer and worship walk'.

2 Handprint prayers for others
5 minutes

What you need
- One of the handprints from *Countdown 3* for each child
- Pens or pencils

What you do
Give out the handprints from *Countdown 3* (intentionally giving everyone someone else's print). Ask the group to think about someone they could reach out to in the coming week. Each person should write a prayer for someone they know who is left out at school or who is sick. Encourage the children to think about how they can help that person this week. Jesus restored the man to full health and a full life. The children will probably not have the opportunity to heal anyone, but what can they do to restore someone who is left out?

Go on to *Activity 3* 'Prayer and worship walk'.

3 Prayer and worship walk
5 minutes

What you need
- Self-portraits and photographs from *Countdown 3*
- Images of children around the world from *Countdown 2*

What you do
Together, stick some of the images from this session around the room, portraits/photographs, images of children and handprint prayers. Walk around the room and look at the pictures, talking about the way in which God has made us all so different yet loves us individually. Come together and suggest ideas for a group prayer for others around the world or those people we know who need prayer. The children may be confident enough to say their own prayers, or the leader could pray on behalf of the group.

Session 2
Caring hands

Countdown 5:

Hands up for fun and games

Choose one or more of these activities (depending on time) to introduce today's theme to your group. They focus on using the senses. In the games that require a blindfold, make sure children are happy to be blindfolded before you start. Whilst playing the games, remind the children how much we use our senses in everyday life. After the games, discuss how difficult it is when we cannot use one of our senses. How do people overcome some of these difficulties today? There may be children within the group who can share their own experiences, or the experiences of friends and family. Ensure this is done sensitively.

 **Sleeping tambourine**
5 minutes

What you need
- Tambourine
- Blindfold

What you do
Ask the children to sit in a circle on the floor. Blindfold a volunteer and guide them to sit in the middle of the circle. A tambourine is carefully passed around the circle, from person to person, without making a sound. If the child in the centre hears a sound, they should point to where they think the sound is coming from. If they are right, they swap places with the person who made the sound.

A variation on the game above can be played using a large bunch of keys or a bag of coins.

 **Feely bag**
⊕ *5 minutes*

What you need
- Bag
- Several objects for the children to guess

What you do
Sit the group in a circle and, out of everyone's view, put one of the objects in the bag. Pass the bag round and ask the children to guess what the object is, just by feeling it. Repeat this task with several different objects. Use a range of objects with different textures and shapes eg pine cone, orange, a marble, a ball of play dough.

3 Navigator
5 minutes

What you need
- Blindfold

What you do
Make sure there are no dangerous obstacles in the way before you begin this challenge! Blindfold one of the children and set the challenge of collecting an object from the other side of the room. The rest of the group should help by shouting out directions. Time the first volunteer, and then allow other children to try to beat that time.

4 Tasty challenge
5 minutes

What you need
- Selection of sweets, eg fruit gums, pastilles or jelly sweets
- Blindfold

Mark 7:31–37
Jesus heals a man who was deaf and could hardly talk

Aim
To recognise the way in which Jesus' hands cared for those who would have been unable to help themselves.

Social justice theme
This session we will start to look at Fairtrade food.

Jesus' extraordinary actions opened up the life of the man who could not hear or talk. He understood the needs of the man and cared enough to help him. We too need to understand the needs of others and empathise with their situations, caring enough to want to help them too.

2

World of a child

Children's fiction is full of heroes who come to the rescue, often using some sort of magical power. Jesus is indeed such a hero, but his power is far more than something magical. Children may know someone who is deaf or blind and will appreciate what it meant to the man when he was completely healed.

What you do
Remember to check if any child has a food allergy before you begin. Blindfold one child who tastes four sweets. Ask them to guess the flavour of each one as they taste it. See how many the child guesses correctly, then challenge other children to be blindfolded and guess.

5 Smelly challenge
5 minutes

What you need
• Range of strong-smelling foods or drinks in containers eg onion, cheese, vinegar, herbs, strawberries, banana

What you do
Remember to check if any child has a food allergy before you begin. Blindfold a volunteer and ask them to guess what the food or drink is, just from the smell. Did they guess correctly? Challenge other children to be blindfolded and guess other food or drink just using their sense of smell.

Countdown 4:

Open the Bible

1 Read the story
5 minutes

What you need
• Bibles or photocopies of page 50

What you do
Sit together in a circle and recap on the story about the man with leprosy from the previous session. What do the children remember? Remind them of the way in which people who were different would have been regarded at that time.

Read the story about the man who was deaf and could hardly talk in Mark 7:31–37. Ask the children to listen out for all the things they think are unusual! After you have read the story, ask the children what unusual things they heard. Some may mention that Jesus put spit on the man's tongue, others that Jesus healed a deaf and mute man! Point out again that Jesus helped a man who had severe problems, and that he had the power to do so. By now, the group will have heard stories of Jesus healing two very different people. They may well be

forming a picture of Jesus in their minds already. Spend some time exploring what the children think of Jesus so far. Read out verse 37 again. This is the crowd's reaction to what Jesus did: '"Everything he does is good!"' What is the group's impression of Jesus? Do they agree with the crowd?

Explore the story further using one or more of the suggestions below:

2 Before and after
10 minutes

What you do
In groups of three or four, act out the reactions of the people who brought the man to Jesus both *before* Jesus healed him and *after* Jesus healed him. Encourage the children to think about how they felt. What do the group think the people said? How would their emotions have changed after Jesus healed their friend? What do the children think the man's friends would have said to Jesus?

If they are willing, ask the groups to show each other what they think happened before and after. Emphasise that no one group is right or wrong, but it is helpful to try and understand the story from different points of view.

3 Video diary
15 minutes

What you need
• Video camera, tape recorder or MP3 player to record the activity (optional)

What you do
Ask the children to work in groups of three. Choose to be either the healed man, Jesus or one of the disciples watching this miracle. Report to a video diary (in the style of those seen on reality TV programmes) about what they saw, heard and felt. Ask the children to rehearse their video diary with each other before performing to the rest of the groups. If a video camera or tape recorder/MP3 player is available, record the diary and share this with the whole group.

Countdown 3:

Keep those hands busy

This section allows the children to continue thinking about their reaction to the Bible story, and to Jesus' actions and compassion. As you work, chat about the story and the group's reaction to it. Be sure to share your own thoughts too.

1 Memory ears and mouths
10 minutes

What you need
- Template from page 55
- Thin card
- Felt-tip pens
- Glue
- Scissors

What you do
Give out the card and the templates and ask each child to decide if they want to make an ear or a mouth. Ask them to draw round and cut out their ear/mouth, and then decorate it. When they have finished, ask them to write 'Everything he does is good!' around the edge of their ear/mouth.

Encourage the children to take the ear/mouth home and put it where they can see it. This will help them remember the story for today and what they have learnt about Jesus so far. Chat for a while about what the children will think of when they see their ear/mouth.

2 Chain reaction
10 minutes

What you need
- Thin strips of brightly coloured paper (about 20 cm x 3 cm)
- Glue
- Felt-tip pens
- Collage materials

What you do
Make a paper chain using brightly coloured strips of paper. Give each child two strips of paper to start with. On one strip the children should write something that stood out for them from today's story. On the other they should write something they can do to care for others. Encourage the group to decorate the other side of the strip with patterns using felt-tip pens or

collage materials. Join all the strips together to make a long chain. Children can carry on making strips for the chain if you have time. Display the paper chain around the room (you may want to use it in *Countdown 1*).

As you work, explain that this is a story chain for this session. You are thinking about the story as well as thinking about what that story means for you.

3 Picture perfect
10 minutes

What you need
- Large sheets of paper
- Felt-tip pens
- Collage materials
- Glue

What you do
Create pictures of what the children think today's story would have looked like. Each person in the group could do their own picture, or you could do one as a group together. As you work, chat about the story and what the children remember. Ask them what the story means for them. Is there anyone that they can help, like Jesus helped the man? Or are they impressed by Jesus' kindness and power?

Countdown 2:

Joining hands around the world

The focus for this session is on fair trade, and will continue in Session 3.

1 Where does it come from?
10 minutes

What you need
- Range of everyday products familiar to the children such as food, clothes, and electronic items which clearly state where they were produced
- Large map of the world
- Sticky dots or OHP pen

What you do
Together, look on the packaging to see where the foods and goods are produced. Using a large map of the world, or one on OHP acetate, locate these countries and mark where the product

2

comes from. Discuss the range of countries that produce the things we use every day.

During the next week, ask the children to look at packaging and labels on things they eat and use. They could bring one item with them to the next session to show the rest of the group.

 **How does it get here?**
10 minutes

What you need
- Images of people involved in the production of the things we use and eat – these can be downloaded from www.fairtrade.org.uk

What you do
Make a sequence of images of people involved in producing the things we use – tea, coffee, bananas. For instance, the worker picks the bananas for the farm owner; they are packaged, transported, delivered to the supermarkets and sold to us.

Discuss how many people are involved in growing, packaging, transporting and selling the things we use. Explain how these people are often exploited and not given a fair wage or adequate working conditions by their bosses, or a fair price for their goods.

Ask the children to look at the packaging and labels of the things they eat and use during the next week. They could then bring one item with them to the next session as a starting point for discussion.

caring person Jesus showed us we should be. The children can read out their paper chains as their prayers for others.

 **Prayers around the world**
10 minutes

What you need
- Sticky notes or small squares of paper (about 6 cm x 6 cm)
- World map
- Map of your local area

What you do
Working individually or in pairs, write prayers on the squares of paper or sticky notes for people around the world, especially those involved in producing food and goods for our use. Place these prayers on the appropriate area of the world map.

The children might want prayer for people they know in their local area – their relatives or friends. There may be people who are ill, and in whose lives they want Jesus to show his power. Write these prayers and stick them on the appropriate place in your local area.

When you have finished, say that you are going to have a time when the children can read out their prayers if they want to. Finish this time by asking Jesus to show his power in these situations. You could read verse 37 to round it off.

Countdown 1:

Hands to praise and hands to pray

Continue to use songs to praise God, see the suggestions on page 7. The song 'Jesus went out of his way' would be appropriate for this session.

 **Paper chain prayers**
10 minutes

What you need
- The paper chain made during *Countdown 3*

What you do
Hold the paper chain and share some of the ways the children had decided to care for others. Either individually, or on behalf of the group, pray for God's help in being the kind of

Session 3
Sharing hands

Countdown 5:

Hands up for fun and games

These games reinforce the importance of sharing resources, which links to the story of Jesus feeding 4,000 people as well as the focus later in the session on fair trade. Choose one or more of these activities (depending on time).

 **Treasure hunt**
5 minutes

What you need
- Gold coins or wrapped sweets

What you do
Remember to check if any child has a food allergy before you begin. Before the session, hide gold coins or sweets around the room. Ask the children to hunt for the sweets, and bring any they find to a central place. If the children need help finding the last few coins, give them a clue by calling 'warm' or 'cold' to indicate how close they are to finding them. When you have all the coins, share them out equally with the group, emphasising that everyone should have a fair share, rather than being allowed to keep all the coins they found themselves.

 **Beanbag relay**
5 minutes

What you need
- 12 beanbags or soft balls
- 12 hoops or buckets
- Prize

What you do
In four teams, run a relay race. The first person has three beanbags to distribute into three hoops or buckets, running with one beanbag at a time. The next person has to collect the three beanbags, one at a time, and bring them back to the team. The next person distributes the beanbags; the next collects them in again until everyone in the team has had a go. The winning team receives a prize on the condition that they have to share it with the whole of the group! (Remember allergies!)

 **Tower challenge**
5 minutes

What you need
- Newspaper
- Four rolls of sticky tape
- Four balls of string
- Four pairs of scissors

What you do
Divide the group into four teams and give them a newspaper, a roll of sticky tape, a ball of string and a pair of scissors. Challenge the teams to build the tallest tower in five minutes. Measure the towers to see which group has won.

Repeat the challenge, this time giving one team a newspaper, sticky tape, string and scissors; one team a newspaper, sticky tape and scissors; one team just newspaper and scissors and the last team just a newspaper.

Who wins the challenge this time? Is that fair? How did it feel to be given fewer resources or more resources than the other teams?

Mark 8:1–10
Jesus feeds 4,000

Aim
To understand how Jesus met the needs of people by feeding a huge group of his listeners. With his hands he shared out the food.

Social justice theme
This session we will continue looking at Fairtrade food.

Once again Jesus showed his compassion for the people he met (verses 2 and 3) and helped them by meeting their immediate physical needs. By looking again at the issue of fair trade, we will explore how we can meet the physical needs of people in practical ways.

3

Countdown 4:

Open the Bible

 Read the story
10 minutes

What you need
- Picnic rugs
- Floor cushions
- Picnic basket
- Loaves of bread
- Fish (or pictures of fish!)
- Bibles or photocopies of page 50

What you do
Set up the environment to tell this story using the picnic equipment you have brought. If possible, take the children outside into a garden area (ensure that you keep to your church's child protection policy). Read the story in Mark 8:1–10, with children reading the parts of the characters and using the props above to enact the story. Ask the children to listen out for what the people needed.

Continue to explore the story using one or more of the suggestions below:

 What do we need?
15 minutes

What you need
- Bibles or photocopies of page 50
- Paper
- Pens

What you do
In groups of two or three make three lists:
1. Things that are essential to make it possible for us to live
2. Things we have to make our lives easier or more comfortable
3. Things that are a luxury
The lists can use words or pictures.

Share the lists and discuss what our basic needs are. How much of what we have are luxuries? How many people do not have their basic needs met? Why is this? What would Jesus think about this?

In the Bible story, what did the people need? What does the story of the feeding of the 4,000 show us about Jesus' attitudes to peoples' needs? Jesus felt sorry for the crowd and wanted to give them what they needed. Note

that Jesus gave the crowd more than they needed!

 Big sum
10 minutes

What you need
- Bibles or photocopies of page 50
- Enlarged photocopy of the sum on page 55
- Marker pen

What you do
Show the enlarged sheet and ask the following questions. Ask a child to fill in the answers.

Begin with the number of days these people were with Jesus.	(3)	3
Add on the number of people there.	(4,000)	4,003
Add on the number of times Jesus told the crowd to sit down.	(1)	4,004
Divide by the number of loaves of bread Jesus took.	(7)	572
Take away the number of times Jesus blessed the food.	(2)	570
Divide by the number of Bible verses that tell this story.	(10)	57
Take away the number of times Jesus told the disciples that he cared for the people.	(1)	56
Divide by the number of this chapter in Mark's Gospel.	(8)	7

(You should be left with the number of baskets of food that were left over!)

Read the Bible story once more and then complete this sum, using the verses to find the answers.

Countdown 3:

Keep those hands busy

The activities for this session continue the picnic theme. These ideas could be used for an outdoor picnic, maybe even a trip to the local park. This will require organisation beforehand to ensure extra adult helpers and completed permission forms. Alternatively, have a fun indoor picnic.

⊙1 Picnic time
✛ *20 minutes*

What you need
- Paper
- Pens or pencils
- Picnic food and drinks

What you do
In pairs, make a list of the items needed for a picnic then make a group list of all the ideas.

Prepare simple picnic food – sandwiches, ice cakes or biscuits, a fruit punch or smoothies, fruit salad. Either the club supplies the food or children's parents could be asked to bring in items from home, reinforcing the idea of 'sharing hands'. As you prepare the food, chat with the children about the story – what do they think about what Jesus did? Jesus was concerned about the crowd and used his power to help them. Let the children ask you questions if they want to. If you don't know the answer, don't panic! Say that you don't know and promise to find out!

Remember to check for food allergies when preparing and eating the food, keeping to health and safety guidelines.

You may want to keep the picnic to eat in *Countdown 1*.

⊙2 Salt dough picnic
15 minutes

What you need
- Flour
- Fine salt
- Water
- Dough tools

What you do
Before the session, mix together 1 cup of flour, 1 cup of salt and about half a cup of water to create a firm dough. Make enough dough for your group. (There are many alternative recipes for salt dough – type 'salt dough recipe' into an Internet search engine to find more.)

Give out the dough to each child and ask them to make some loaves of bread and some small fish. As you work together, chat about the story and about how Jesus performed a miracle to meet the needs of the people around him. What do the children think about that? Make sure you share your own thoughts too!

When you've finished, put the loaves and fish to one side. If you have the facilities and can do so safely, bake your salt dough objects at 180 °C

for about 20 minutes. Baking times will vary depending on the size and thickness of the object, but make sure that all of it is hard.

Countdown 2:

Joining hands around the world

⊙1 Fairtrade picnic
5 minutes

What you need
- Fairtrade products eg fruit, chocolate

What you do
Remember to check for food allergies before you taste anything! Recap on the fair trade focus from the previous week. Show the children some of the Fairtrade products you have collected and talk about the labels that they may have looked out for since the last session. If they have brought some from the last session as requested make sure you mention this.

Chat about what the children like, and what they have never tried. If you have Internet access, explore products highlighted at www.fairtrade.org.uk/products.htm and maybe even try one or two of the recipes, if time and facilities allow. Otherwise, have a tasting session of the food you have brought in.

What do the children think of buying Fairtrade products? Think together of ways they can make a difference. (Be sensitive, though, as many Fairtrade products are slightly more expensive than their non-Fairtrade counterparts. Parents may not be pleased if their children go home demanding that they buy the more expensive product!)

⊙2 Fairtrade resources
 *5 minutes*

What you need
- Fairtrade publicity materials from www.fairtrade.org.uk
- Paper
- Art materials

What you do
Recap on the fair trade focus from the previous week and the labels the children may have discovered. Share out the posters and leaflets for the children to look at during the session and take home. Challenge them to design a

3

fair trade poster to be displayed in the church. Maybe a Fairtrade bar of chocolate could be offered as the prize! Once the children have finished, pin the posters up around your room.

Countdown 1:

Hands to praise and hands to pray

Continue to use songs to praise God, see the suggestions on page 7. You could sing 'Who took fish and bread?' to follow the theme for this session.

 Shared picnic (1)
10 minutes

What you need
- Prepared picnic from *Countdown 3*

What you do
In the story of the feeding of the 4,000, Jesus took the loaves and blessed them. Remind the children of this, and then take the food prepared for the picnic and the Fairtrade products and say thank you to God for providing them. Ask the children if there's anything else they'd like to say thank you to God for providing. Say thank you for these things too!

Finally… enjoy the picnic! If you eat the picnic earlier in the session, adapt this prayer suggestion.

 Salt dough prayers
5 minutes

What you need
- Salt dough items from *Countdown 3*

What you do
Sit in a circle and give out the salt dough items. Be careful if you haven't baked these, as they might still be pliable! Ask the children to hold their item in their hands and thank God for providing the food they eat every day. Then ask everyone to pass their item on to the person to their left. Holding their new item, pray for either an area in the world where there isn't enough food, or for one of the producers they learnt about in *Countdown 2*. Pass the items round again and ask them to thank Jesus that he meets the needs of people everywhere.

Ensure that the children don't try and eat the salt dough!

Session 4
Welcoming hands

Countdown 5:

Hands up for fun and games

Choose one or more of these activities (depending on time) to introduce today's theme to your group.

The opposites game
5 minutes

What you do

This game is played like 'Simon Says' but whatever Simon says to do, the children have to do the opposite eg Simon says, 'Stand up,' and the children have to sit down, Simon says, 'Turn left,' and the children have to turn right.

Remind the children that Jesus often said things or behaved in ways that were the opposite of what people expected. He cared for those who were usually ignored, and welcomed those who were usually turned away.

High Five sports day
15 minutes

What you need

- A range of objects for mini-challenges eg balloons, balls, hoops

What you do

Before the session, decide on a few silly challenges which all the children can take part in. Collect together the necessary equipment and set up the challenges for a **High Five** sports day!

Challenges could include a relay race with a balloon between the legs, a three-legged race, a race balancing a book on the head, a 'limbo' challenge. The challenges should be fun with a slightly silly feel!

When you have finished, congratulate the winners of all the challenges and discuss whether the challenges showed who was the greatest in the group. Be affirming as you chat, pointing out that everyone has different talents.

Medals ceremony
⊕ *5 minutes*

What you need

- Prepared medals made of gold card and ribbon or certificates (computer-generated or hand drawn)

What you do

Stage an award ceremony where everyone receives a medal or small prize for some achievement such as being a good sport, thinking of others, working as a team, having a warm smile. This could follow on from the mini-sports day or be awards for general attitudes towards each other in the club in the first three sessions. The important thing is that everyone receives an award for some achievement involving others and that you affirm all the children for something they have achieved or something that they do. The point should be made that everybody is special and has something to contribute to the group. All the children should be recognised for one of their special qualities.

Countdown 4:

Open the Bible

The look on their faces
15 minutes

What you need

- Bibles or photocopies of page 51

Mark 9:33–37
Who is the greatest?

Aim
To understand that Jesus welcomed people with outstretched hands (maybe not always literally), however insignificant or important they were.

Social justice theme
This session we will be thinking about children without choices.

Jesus turns the idea of being the greatest on its head and gives some revolutionary teaching in this passage. He also showed that he was not too important to spend time with children. He wants us to be welcoming in the same way.

4

We live in a very competitive world where those that come out top get noticed. There are some exceptions to this, such as schools running non-competitive sports activities. The reality is that some children will know they are winners but others will have low self-esteem and perceive themselves as losers. This story emphasises that, in God's eyes, we all have value! He welcomes us all. This may be a surprising message for some children who are struggling at home – that Jesus welcomes them, even though they are 'only' children.

- Paper
- Pencils
- Coloured pencils or felt-tip pens

What you do

Ask the children to listen as you read Mark 9:33–37. Then organise the children to take the parts of Jesus, a child and the disciples and read through the story again, with everyone acting out their parts. This is a short story so you could act it out more than once.

Ask the children to draw a quick sketch of the look on the disciples' faces and, on the other side of the paper, draw how the child would have looked when Jesus put his arm around them.

You will need to tell them that, at the time of Jesus, children were not really seen as important so the disciples might have been shocked by what Jesus did. Talk about how things are different today, but are there ways that the children still feel they are not important? How might the children in the story have felt? What important message was Jesus giving the disciples?

Remind the children that Jesus was talking about what it meant to be great and about being a servant. In welcoming someone else, we are in effect welcoming Jesus himself. Link this to the games played at the beginning of the session. The awards were given not for sporting success, but for attitudes. The opposites game required the children to do something different from what was usually expected. Jesus was doing exactly that.

Continue to unpack the story by exploring one of the following:

⏱2 Who is the greatest?
10 minutes

What you need

- Selection of magazines with pictures of celebrities: pop stars, film stars, sporting heroes

What you do

Sit in a circle and talk about who the greatest people are, and why. Provide some pictures from magazines of celebrities and sports stars. What is so special about them? How do we decide who is the greatest? Make a list of all the criteria we might use to describe someone as great.

Read the story again of Jesus welcoming children. His values were the opposite of those of his day: to have a place of honour, you need

to be a servant; to be the greatest, you need to become like a child. Link this to the games played at the beginning of the session.

These are revolutionary attitudes Jesus is calling us to, so be ready to chat with the children about any questions they have. Can they think how these attitudes might affect their daily life?

⏱3 Learn and remember challenge
5 minutes

What you need

- An acetate or large sheet of paper
- Marker pen
- Smaller pieces of paper

What you do

Before the session, write: Jesus said, "If you want the place of honour, you must become a slave and serve others!" Mark 9:35, onto a large sheet of paper, but missing out all the vowels. Play the word game 'Hangman' to complete this learn and remember verse. (You could make it more difficult by missing out more letters.)

Once you have completed the verse, cover up more and more of the words until the children can say this verse without having it written out in front of them. Make sure they understand what it is that Jesus is saying. Come back to this at the end of the session and also at the start of the next session.

Countdown 3:

Keep those hands busy

Continue to chat with the group as you work together on these craft activities. The idea that we should serve others rather than look to be the best will be an unusual idea for both churched and non-churched children, so they may have lots of questions about it!

🔧1 Make a medal
⊕ *20 minutes*

What you need

- Quick drying clay or cardboard
- Ribbon
- Gold or silver paint or gold or silver paper
- Glue
- Scissors

• Blunt pencil

What you do

Make a medal for someone in the group or at home using quick drying clay or cardboard. The award should be given for the 'Greatest —' and should be about someone's attitudes and actions, not talent or success such as, Greatest Friend, Greatest Helper, Greatest Encourager. A large number 1 or smiley face could be carved into the clay before it sets. If you have time, come back to the activity once the medals have dried and paint them gold or silver.

Alternatively, cut out a cardboard disc and cover it with gold or silver paper. A large number 1 or smiley face could be pressed into the disc using a blunt pencil to give the impression of an embossed medal!

Ask the children to share who their medal is for and why they are awarding it. Continue to talk about Jesus' definition of true greatness.

 **Make a certificate**
20 minutes

What you need
• Coloured A4 paper
• Felt-tip pens
• Gold and silver pens

What you do

Make a certificate for someone in the group or at home using A4 coloured paper. The award should be given for the 'Greatest —' (as in *Activity 1* above). The certificate should state who and what the award is for. Decorate it with patterns and pictures. If a computer is available, the certificate could be designed on a computer. As in *Activity 1*, ask everyone in the group who they are giving their certificate to, and continue to talk about Jesus' definition of true greatness.

 **Welcome sign**
20 minutes

What you need
• Long piece of paper (old wallpaper is ideal)
• Pictures of people cut from magazines and catalogues
• Glue
• Scissors
• Felt-tip pens or paint

What you do

Work together to make a 'welcome' sign for your club. Write 'welcome' in large letters right across the banner and then stick pictures cut from magazines all around the letters. The pictures should include people of all ages, colours, sizes and shapes. Use lots of bright colour to make your banner bold and welcoming. Stick it in a place where everyone can see.

If you have a large group, you could make more than one banner.

 **Door hanger**
20 minutes

What you need
• Door hanger template from page 56
• Thin coloured card or craft foam
• Felt-tip pens
• A laminator or sticky-backed plastic (optional)

What you do

Give out copies of the door hanger template from page 56 and either craft foam or cardboard. Make a door hanger with the words of the Learn and remember challenge from *Countdown 4* on it to place on the children's doors at home. Decorate the door hanger using felt-tip pens. Cardboard door hangers could be laminated or covered in sticky-backed plastic to make them more durable.

4

Countdown 2:

Joining hands around the world

The concept of human trafficking is a sensitive issue to be introduced to children, and some aspects are not appropriate to share with children of this age. The issues of human trafficking will instead be explored under the title of 'children without choices'.

 1 Children without choices
10 minutes

What you need
- Images of children (available from the Salvation Army International Department www.salvationarmy.org.uk/id)
- Large sheet of paper
- Marker pen

What you do
Discuss with the children the importance of making choices. What kind of choices are they free to make every day? Ask them to share their ideas in pairs before sharing as a group. Gather everyone's suggestions together and write them down on a sheet of paper.

Show the children images of children who are not free to make their own choices but are forced to work in unsafe conditions and are exploited by adults. What emotions do we see on the faces of the children in the pictures? Brainstorm some ideas and write them on the other side of your sheet of paper. Discuss how this fits with Jesus' view of children. Think about what Jesus was showing about children. How does the importance he placed on children challenge what is happening to these children?

 2 Real choices
5 minutes

What you need
- Images of children (available from the Salvation Army International Department www.salvationarmy.org.uk/id)
- Signs saying A, B and C
- List of up to ten questions

What you do
At one end of the room, stick up the three signs with the letters A, B and C. Ask the children to stand at the other end. Read out a question about real-life choices the children have to

make and ask the children to choose answer A, B or C by running to the appropriate letter. Once they have decided, give them one more opportunity to change their mind. Repeat this for the rest of the questions.

The questions should deal with choices the children make every day, such as decisions at school, with friends and families, without there necessarily being a right or wrong answer. The children have to choose one of the options. For example: You are given maths homework on Friday. Do you a) do your homework as soon as you get home from school; b) set aside time to do your homework on Sunday; c) do it with a friend on Saturday? Or: What would you prefer for breakfast a) a boiled egg; b) a bowl of sugar puffs; c) two slices of toast? Or: Your school is changing the colour of its uniform. Would you like it to be a) red; b) blue; c) black?

Show the children images of children who are not free to make their own choices but are forced to work in unsafe conditions and are exploited by adults. Remember that this is an activity about the privilege of having the freedom to make choices rather than making the 'right' decisions.

Countdown 1:

Hands to praise and hands to pray

Use the song suggestions on page 7 in a time of singing with the group. The Scripture Union CDs *Light for Everyone* (978 1 84427 080 4) and *Reach Up!* (978 1 84427 169 6) both have a good selection of non-confessional songs to use with non-churched children. You could try using 'Anyone can come to God' from *Reach Up!*

 1 North, south, east and west
10 minutes

What you need
- Chalk or masking tape

What you do
Mark out a giant compass on your floor using either chalk or masking tape, clearly marking on north, south, east and west.

Walk to the north and pray for the children in that part of the world, mentioning a few countries in the north. Older children may be able to suggest several countries. You could ask four good readers to read the following prayer out loud at each compass point:

4

Dear God, we pray for children who live in the north/south/east/west especially those in
_____. Help them to recognise all the good things you have given them.
We pray for children who aren't able to make their own choices because adults do not give them any freedom and treat them as if they are not important.
May they know that Jesus loves them. He knows they are important.
Amen.

Repeat for east, south and west. The leader or the children could pray for children around the world – for their safety, for their health, for food and safe drinking water, for fair working conditions, for education.

⊙2 Catch the world

10 minutes

What you need
- An inflatable globe

What you do
Standing in a circle, throw an inflatable globe to each other. Each child who catches the globe has the opportunity to pray for children in a part of the world that they choose or can find on the globe. They could use this sentence:

Dear God, please care for the children in
_____.

If a child does not want to pray out loud, they can throw the globe to another child who has not yet caught it.

5

Session 5
Giving hands

Mark 10:17–31;
Mark 12:41–44
A rich man, and a
widow's offering

Aim
To understand that
Jesus expects us to give,
but it is our *attitude* in
giving that counts, not
really how *much* we
give. Jesus came
ultimately to give his
own life!

Social justice theme
This session we will
continue to think about
children without
choices.

The rich man loved his
possessions. The poor
woman gave all that
she could. The session
will consider ways in
which our giving can
help others.

Countdown 5:

Hands up for fun and games

Choose one or more of these activities
(depending on time) to introduce today's theme
to your group.

▍1 Thread a needle
 *5 minutes*

What you need
- Large-eyed needles
- Thin thread and thick wool

What you do
Attempt to thread a large needle with thin
thread, and then try with thick thread or wool.
Provide several of these so that all children are
able to have a go. How difficult is it to do this?
(Ensure that the children are careful with the
point on the needle. If necessary, put some Blu-
tack or Plasticine on the end.) How difficult
would it be to thread a camel through the eye
of a needle? Explain that you are going to look
at how hard it is sometimes to give, harder than
actually going through the eye of a needle!

▍2 Obstacle course
5 minutes

What you need
- Items for the children to climb over, under
  and through

What you do
Consider health and safety issues carefully
before the children take part in this activity.
Organise the children into four teams. Set up a
range of obstacles for the teams to climb over,
under and through. Pop-up tunnels and hoops
are particularly good for this activity, but

obstacles could be improvised out of chairs and
tables. The children should race against each
other in relay teams. Talk about how difficult
this was. Explain that in this session you will be
looking at how difficult it is to give generously.

▍3 Carrying race
5 minutes

What you need
- Objects for the children to carry (cushions or
  empty boxes are ideal for this activity)

What you do
Choose two of the children to walk from
starting point (A) to finishing point (B). Then ask
the children to repeat the exercise carrying one
object, then two, then three and so on until one
of the children drops one or more of the objects.
Allow other children to have a go at the same
activity. The winner is the person who managed
to get from A to B carrying the most objects
without dropping them. Talk about how
difficult this was. Explain that in this session you
are going to look at how difficult it is to give
generously.

Countdown 4:

Open the Bible

▍1 What happened next (1)?
15 minutes

What you need
- Bibles or photocopies of page 51
- Sheet of paper or acetate and pen
- OHT of page 57

What you do

Read the story of the rich man in Mark 10:17–31 to the end of verse 21, as marked with *. As you read, show each picture from the cartoon strip on page 57. Ask the children, in twos or threes, to act out what they think happened next. Remind them that this man was a very good, clever and important man. He expected Jesus to say he was doing OK. Let the groups show each other what they thought might happen next then give out the copies of the story and read to the end together. Were the children surprised at what Jesus said? Why did the man go away sad?

Seated in a circle, talk about the things Jesus said in previous stories that the children have looked at in **High Five**. Remind them about the way Jesus often spoke in the opposite way to what people might have expected.

Read Mark 12:41–44, showing the cartoon strip illustrations on page 57 as you do so. Make two columns on a sheet of paper/acetate. Ask the children to call out words about the rich man and write them in one column, and, in the other, write down words about the poor woman whom no one thought was important. Compare the words in the different columns. So who was pleasing Jesus more – the woman or the rich man?

Jesus knows what makes us do things, our motivation. Talk about whether that is a scary or a good concept. Be prepared to give an example from your own life about how attitudes count! We can hide nothing from God.

 **What happened next (2)?**
15 minutes

What you need

- Bibles or photocopies of page 51
- Sheet of paper or acetate and pen

What you do

This activity is the reverse of *Activity 1*. Read from Mark 12:41–44 as far as the end of verse 42. Ask the children, in twos or threes, to act out what they think happened next, reminding them of how unimportant this woman was. Widows at the time of Jesus were often really poor because they had no one to support them or bring in any money to buy food. Let the groups show each other what they thought might happen next then give out the copies of the story and read to the end. Were the children surprised about what Jesus said?

Seated in a circle, talk about the things Jesus said in previous stories that the children have looked at in **High Five**. Remind them about the

way Jesus often spoke in the opposite way to what people might have expected.

Read together the story of the rich man from Mark 10:17–31. Make two columns on a sheet of paper/acetate. Ask the children to call out words about the rich man and write them in one column. In the other, write down words about the people who give up things to follow Jesus (verses 28–31). Compare the words in the different columns. What do the children think Jesus means when he says that it's hard for rich people to be his friend? What do children think about the meaning of verse 29, when Jesus talks about people who have given up their home or family?

Countdown 3:

Keep those hands busy

All of the items made in this session can be used later as part of the focus on praise and prayer in *Countdown 1*. As you work together, talk about the attitudes of the rich man and the widow in the Bible story. Chat about how the children spend their money and the ways in which they give to others. Be sure to share your own thoughts too.

 **Gift tag**
10 minutes

What you need

- Scissors
- Small rectangles of thin, coloured card
- Felt-tip pens
- Collage materials
- Glue
- Hole punch
- Ribbon

What you do

Fold the card in half to make gift tags. Punch a hole in one end and thread ribbon through it. Decorate one side of the gift tag to be used in the prayer time (*Countdown 1*) at the end of the session.

As you do this together, talk about how the children spend their money and the ways in which they give to others. Remind them about the story of the rich man and the story of the poor widow. One couldn't give up their money because they had so much of it. The other gave a little, but it was all she had. Remind the group that it is all about attitude. If you have money,

5

you should be willing to give it away if you need to. The rich man liked his money too much!

 **Money box**
20 minutes

What you need
• Money box template from page 58
• Thin, coloured card
• Felt-tip pens
• Paint
• Collage materials
• Glue

What you do
Draw around the template onto card and cut out the money box net. Remember to cut a slot in the lid for the money to go in! Decorate using paints, felt-tip pens or collage materials. Fold along the lines and glue the flaps in place.

As you do this together, talk about how the children spend their money and the ways in which they give to others.

 **Make a purse**
20 minutes

What you need
• Square of fabric 20 cm x 20 cm
• PVA glue or needle and thread
• Sequins, buttons and scraps of fabric
• Velcro (optional)

What you do
Make a simple purse using an 'envelope' of fabric. Fold a third of the fabric over from the bottom and sew or glue down the two edges. Then fold over the top third to form a closing flap. You could use Velcro to fasten the flap to the purse. Decorate with sequins, collage materials or shapes cut out of other fabric stuck or sewn on the outside.

As you do this together, talk about how the children spend their money and the ways in which they give to others.

 # Countdown 2:
Joining hands around the world

Recap on the topic introduced in the previous session, 'children without choices'.

 **Children without choices DVD**
10 minutes

What you need
• DVD player, television or computer
• Anti-trafficking DVD produced by The Salvation Army International Development Department (www.salvationarmy.org.uk)

What you do
Watch the DVD with the children. Ask them to talk in pairs about what they have just seen.

Decide on three things they have learnt from the DVD that they did not know before. Share these three things with the whole group. It may be helpful to watch the DVD again after the discussion as reinforcement.

UN Rights of the Child
10 minutes

What you need
• Felt-tip pens
• Plain paper
• Photocopies of the UN Rights of the Child, see a simplified version on page 59.

What you do
Give each pair a photocopy of the extract from the Declaration of the Rights of the Child from page 59. Invite the children to think about what this declaration is saying about children. Talk about examples in their own lives where these rights are allowed, and the people who enable these to happen: such as the right to be educated, or the importance of a name. For many children in the world these rights do not all exist.

Encourage each child to design an A4 poster to promote the UN Rights of the Child. Each poster could take one aspect to publicise and could be taken home to be completed. However, you may like to keep a few back as they are needed for Session 7.

Younger children can write their own name in bubble writing (or can be helped to do so) on a poster and can then decorate this. As they do so, remind them how fortunate they are to have a name as well as being able to go to school.

Remind the children of what Jesus thought about children (Session 4).

Note that the references to parents are not included here. That is not because this is unimportant but that a child who does not benefit from good parenting cannot do anything about it for themselves. It might be unhelpful for them to be part of a discussion on parental responsibility. The principles on page 59 are on issues that a child can identify with. To find out more type: 'Rights of the child' into a search engine.

Countdown 1:

Hands to praise and hands to pray

Continue to sing to praise and worship God, using the suggestions on page 7. Don't introduce too many songs, but concentrate on a range of three or four which the children can learn and enjoy singing.

 1 Gift tag prayers
10 minutes

What you need
- Gift tags made in *Countdown 3* or commercially made gift tags
- Pens

What you do
Use gift tags made earlier or give the children a pre-made gift tag on which they could write a prayer for the children without choices. What would they wish to give to these children if they could? Share these gift prayers together. The prayers could be hung up somewhere during the prayer time, on a washing line across the room, or on some bare tree twigs.

2 Money box promises
10 minutes

What you need
- Money boxes or purses made in *Countdown 3*
- Small pieces of paper
- Pens

What you do
Consider what things the children could 'give up' in order that the money could be used for causes that meet the needs of children. This might include giving up sweets or not buying comics to save the money they would have spent. The money could be collected in the money boxes and purses that the children have made and brought into the final session. In the light of this session, it is important to stress that it is not so much the amount of money but the attitude to giving that really counts.

Encourage the children to write their pledges on a small piece of paper that could be placed inside the money box or purse, to be taken home.

A leader prays out loud for the children you have talked about and seen in this session.

If you are going to launch a fund-raising event, make sure that the children know about it, as well as their parents.

A RIGHT TO EDUCATION

6

Session 6
Loving hands

**Mark 10:32–45;
Mark 12:28–34**

The request of James and John, and the most important commandment: to love God and others

Aim

To recognise that loving God and loving others are the two most important commandments.

Social justice theme
This session we look at water conservation, giving examples of the way in which we can help others in our world.

Jesus makes a clear connection between loving God and loving others. As much as we try, we cannot keep these commandments, but Jesus knows that, and has done something about it through his own death and resurrection. By his Spirit, he then helps us to love both God and others.
James and John assumed they would be accepted by Jesus simply by asking. He made it clear that it was more difficult than that. How could they suffer as he was about to? And had they loved God and others as God wants?

Countdown 5:

Hands up for fun and games

The activities below link to the focus on water later in the session. Choose one or more of them (depending on time).

 **Balancing relay races**
10 minutes

What you need
• Objects to balance on head eg quoits, beanbags, children's buckets

What you do
Organise the children into four relay teams. The teams should race against each other, balancing objects on their head, such as quoits, beanbags or empty buckets. Variations on this game could include balancing objects whilst crossing a simple obstacle course, or balancing objects on the head whilst carrying objects in either hand. (Take into consideration health and safety.)

 **Water relay races**
10 minutes

What you need
• Eight children's buckets
• Water

What you do
These games should be played outside due to the hazard of spilling water on indoor floor surfaces. Organise the children into four relay teams. Carry a small bucket of water to the other side of the course and back to the next person in the team without spilling any. The team with the most water left in the bucket wins.

Variations on this game could include carrying water across a simple obstacle course or carrying two buckets.

 **Water, water everywhere**
😀 *5 minutes*

What you need
• Pens
• Paper

What you do
In pairs, make a list of 10 things we use water for every day; 10 activities that take place in water; 10 places where water can be found; 10 river names; 10 seas or oceans; 10 lakes etc. Each time, the winning pair will be the children who complete their list the quickest. Share the lists and emphasise the importance of water in each of our lives. Make sure that your groups contain a mixed ability of children and leaders. Alternatively, you could make the lists in the same way but the winners are those with the most original ideas rather than the quickest. Each team can read out their list and gain points for items that no one else has written down.

Countdown 4:

Open the Bible

If you have time, do both these activities since they cover both aspects of the theme of this session.

 **Read the story**
20 minutes

What you need
• Bibles or photocopies of page 52
• Video camera (optional)

6

What you do

Explain that Jesus, who had preached to crowds and shown God's love to others in so many ways, had made a lot of enemies in the process. Some people did not like the fact that Jesus said that no one could live a perfect life. The rich man discovered that (see Session 5). Jesus knew that the poor woman's heart was right with God. She pleased him by giving just a little, from the heart.

Read the introduction to the story of James and John in Mark 10:32–34, asking the children to listen out for what Jesus said was going to happen to him.

Then read out the rest of the story of James and John, from Mark 10:35–45, as a play. Once the children have heard the story, choose two children to be James and John, one to be their mother, one to be Jesus and a few to be the other disciples. Read this again, pausing to let the children act out the emotions of the story – a demanding mother, smug James and John, angry disciples, patient and sad Jesus. If possible, video the dramatisation of the story and show it to the group.

Jesus was saying that James and John would not win approval and sit with him in heaven because of anything they had done or asked. It was all about serving others. And Jesus had become the most extreme example of this, something no one else could ever do. He had become a slave and had given his life to rescue people.

Look at the Bible story and ask the children to put verse 45 in their own words. Explain that Jesus knew he was going to die and in a sense was doing a swap, dying in the place of everyone else. He did not deserve to die for he had done nothing wrong. Instead he was prepared to serve others by dying in their place.

If you have time, continue with *Activity 2*.

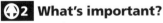 2 What's important?
10 minutes

What you need
- Bibles or photocopies of page 52
- Acetate or large sheet of paper
- Pen

What you do

Before the session, write out the words of Mark 12:30,31 onto acetate or a large sheet of paper. Gather the children together and explain that a wise man was impressed by Jesus so he asked Jesus an important question: 'What is the most important commandment?' How would the children answer that? If a churched child immediately says something like, 'Loving Jesus or God,' ask for other responses. Read Mark 12:28,29.

Jesus gave two commandments which the children are going to learn by creating signs for the key words. This will not necessarily be in BSL or Makaton signs but whatever they can devise. If you get several suggestions, discuss which one is the best. For 'soul' you may come up with a sign for something that is inside us, the real us, that which can respond to God. The sign for 'Jesus' could be pointing to a nail print in the palm of both hands. 'God' could be clasping three fingers of one hand in the other (as Trinity) then sweeping the holding hand upwards.

Read out Mark 12:30,31 and then see what signs the children suggest. Practise this until the children have learnt and understood what Jesus was saying. In the process, talk about how difficult it is to keep these two commandments. In fact, no one can. Only Jesus has ever been able to do that. That is why the Bible says that we have all gone wrong. We all need God's forgiveness. You will be exploring this more in the next two sessions.

Talk about what it means to love others as we love ourselves. How far do we find this difficult or easy? (It is easier for children to understand sin in terms of not loving others than it is to understand sin as not loving God.)

Countdown 3:

Keep those hands busy

Use the time you spend working together on these craft activities to chat about the two most important commandments. What do the children think about loving God and loving others as much as they love themselves?

1 Heart montage
20 minutes

What you need
- Large heart shape cut out of cardboard
- Scissors
- Glue
- Felt-tip pens
- Pictures of all sorts of people in magazines, newspapers and catalogues (these could even include photographs of the children

World of a child

All people have a desire to win the approval of others. You will have already been aware of this with some of the children in the club. This is most marked in our desire to win God's approval. All faiths apart from Christianity have an element of doing good things in order to gain acceptance from God. The Christian faith, however, turns this on its head by declaring that we are all sinners and none of us is able to win God's approval. Only Jesus' death and resurrection can make that possible.

Over the course of **High Five**, children will have become aware of the many good things they can do, all of which are important. They will also have become aware of the effects of sin in the world. Pray for opportunities to make this clear in this session.

6

themselves depending on the photo policy of the church)

What you do

In groups of two or three, make a heart montage. Using a large heart shape pre-cut out of cardboard, cover one side in pictures of people of all ages cut out of magazines and newspapers. On the other side, write in large lettering, 'Love God. Love others.' Decorate this. In a larger group, children could do this activity on their own, or in twos or threes.

2 Salt dough hearts
20 minutes

What you need

- Salt dough (see recipe on page 27)
- Dough tools (or blunt pencils)
- Ribbon
- Poster paints or powder paint mixed with PVA glue
- Baking facilities

What you do

Encourage the children each to shape a heart out of salt dough and decorate it with patterns with the dough tools before baking. Remember to put a hole through the salt dough heart, near the top, so that it can be hung up with a ribbon or piece of string once it has been baked hard and painted. As you do this, talk about how we can love God and how we can love others. Share from your own experience.

If you have time and the right facilities, you could bake the hearts in the same session, or send them home to be baked ready to be decorated in the next session. If you do this you'll need to hand out instructions for baking to the parents (type 'salt dough recipe' into an Internet search engine).

3 Heart wall hanging
20 minutes

What you need

- Thin card
- Ribbon or twine
- Paint, felt-tip pens or collage materials
- Glue
- Scissors
- Templates from page 60, 61

What you do

Make a wall hanging by decorating hearts or people made of cardboard. The heart or people shapes could begin large and get smaller, decorated with paint, felt-tip pens or collage materials. A card saying, 'You must love the Lord your God with all your heart, soul, mind and strength,' should be attached to the top of the wall hanging, and a card saying, 'Love others as much as you love yourself,' attached to the bottom. As you do this, talk about how we can love God and how we can love others. Share from your own experience.

Countdown 2:

Joining hands around the world

1 Introducing *Watershed*
 *10 minutes*

What you need

- *Watershed* DVD produced by the Salvation Army International Development Department (www.salvationarmy.org.uk)
- DVD player or computer

What you do

Watch the *Watershed* DVD together. Discuss in pairs, and then share in groups, the ways in which the children could be involved in saving water, and not wasting it. Explain how every attempt we make to save water helps us all to use the earth's resources wisely. Every little helps. Just because we live in a country where clean water is easily available does not mean that we should take this for granted or waste it unnecessarily.

2 Raindrops
10 minutes

What you need

- Raindrop shaped pieces of paper or plain paper with raindrop shaped template
- Pens

What you do

Provide lots of raindrop shaped pieces of paper, or provide templates for the children to cut out their own raindrop shapes. Write on the raindrops ways in which the children and their families could be involved in saving water, for example: turning off the tap whilst cleaning teeth; having a shower instead of a bath; only boiling as much water in a kettle as is needed. Ask the children to fill in as many raindrops as possible. Place all the raindrops on the floor or on a wall to show that one drop of water on its own is not much, but put together with lots of other drops makes a whole sea of water. On our own, our attempts to save water do not seem much, but if everybody tried then we could make a difference.

Countdown 1:

Hands to praise and hands to pray

If you have sung together in previous sessions, continue to do so now. 'Love the Lord' from *Bitesize Bible Songs* **(978 1 84427 260 0) would fit the theme well. Otherwise, try one or two of these activities:**

 **Love God, love others prayers**
5 minutes

What you need
• The copy of Mark 12:30,31 from *Countdown 4*

What you do
Jesus said, 'You must love the Lord your God with all your heart, soul, mind and strength. Love others as much as you love yourself' Mark 12:30,31. Together, remind each other of the signs that you created for this Learn and remember verse in *Countdown 4*.

Ask all the children to stand up and look upwards with their arms in the air. The leader says the following words:

Lord God, help us to love you with all our heart, soul, mind and strength. Forgive us when we don't do this. (Ask the children to be silent for a few seconds and speak with God.)

Ask all the children to hold out open arms looking towards one another. Say these words:

Lord God, help us to love others as much as we love ourselves. Forgive us when we don't do this. (Ask the children to be silent and ask God to help one other person in the room who needs his help or thank God for one other person in the room.)

 **Paper people prayers**
10 minutes

What you need
• Strips of paper 40 cm x 15 cm
• Scissors
• Pens

What you do
Make a people paper chain by folding the paper several times and cutting the shape of a person along the fold. Write the names of people the children would like to pray for on each paper person. This could be done individually or as a group. Individual people chains could be joined together and hung around the room, or taken home as a reminder for the children to pray for these people throughout the week.

7

Session 7
Hurting hands

Mark 14:43–52; Mark 15:24–28,33–37
Jesus is nailed to a cross

Aim
To understand that throughout his life Jesus changed people's lives. To understand that Jesus loves us so much that he died on the cross with nails hammered through his hands (or wrists).

Social justice theme
Change one thing! This session we're looking at the 'Change One Thing' campaign.

Jesus died to take our place for the things we have done wrong. He changed things for ever, making it possible for people to know God in a new way, including the children who are at **High Five**.

Countdown 5:

Hands up for fun and games

Choose one or more of these activities (depending on time) to introduce today's theme to your group.

1 All change Pictionary
10 minutes

What you need
- Names or pictures of things that change such as: baby to a grown up; caterpillar to a butterfly; bulb to a flower; eggs/flour to a cake; tadpole to a frog; sunset to darkness written on separate pieces of paper
- Pieces of paper and pens

What you do
Put the children in groups around the room, while the leader stands in the centre. One child from each group comes to the leader and is shown the first change. Without speaking they need to draw the thing that changes and the thing it changes into, and the others in the group need to guess both things. Once they have done this, another child from each group tells the leader the answer and is given another change.

The first group to complete all the changes wins. Talk about other changes the children can think of and tell them that today you are going to look at changes that affected Jesus' life.

2 Changed lives
10 minutes

What you need
- Cards with one of the following story titles written down on each: Man with leprosy healed (Mark 1:40–45) Session 1; Deaf/mute man can hear and speak (Mark 7:31–37) Session 2; Hungry crowd full up (Mark 8:1–10) Session 3

What you do
Divide the children into groups of four or five. Give each group one of the cards and, if necessary, copies of the Bible verses that were used in the relevant sessions. Ask them to mime the story, emphasising the way that the men or the crowd were changed as a result of meeting Jesus.

Each group then performs their mime for the others to guess which story it is. Tell them that today you are going to look at other changes that happened in Jesus' life.

Countdown 4:

Open the Bible

1 Hear the story
15 minutes

What you need
- Bibles or photocopies of page 53

What you do
Part one
Explain that Jesus had gone with his friends to a garden. He knew his enemies were planning his death. Ask the children to close their eyes and imagine that it is night-time. Slowly read Mark 14:43–52 to the children, asking them to imagine they are there. Ask the following questions:

How would you feel if you had been watching all this happen?
Why do you think everyone ran away and left Jesus?

How might Jesus have felt when Judas came up and kissed him? (He already knew Judas would betray him.)
What words would you use to describe this event?
What changes have taken place for Jesus and his friends?

Part two
Put the children in groups and give them a copy of the Bible verses and a highlighter pen.

Ask them to mark on the second story from Mark 15:24–37 what all the people there might have heard, tasted, seen, touched or smelt. They can write around the verses any other comments they have about how people's senses were affected. Younger children may need to be helped with this.

What changes had now taken place for Jesus and his friends?

Explain that Jesus' death was not an accident. From the last session you will have seen that Jesus knew this would happen and that it was planned. You could remind the children of this, especially Mark 10:45 which they may have tried to put into their own words. Jesus' death would change the whole world for ever, because he forgave us all our wrongdoing, and death was not the end; Jesus came alive again. (You need to tell the children a little about the resurrection in case there are some who will not be with you for the final session and who do not know the end of the story – which is highly likely with children from a non-churched background.)

⏻2 Watch the story
15 minutes (if you have time)

What you need
- DVD portraying the story of Jesus' death
- DVD player or computer

What you do
If you have time, watch a DVD of the story of the death of Jesus told in a child-accessible way (such as Scripture Union' *Marking Time*, or the *Storykeepers* or *The Miracle Maker*). You might want to watch it beforehand to check its suitability. Discuss what happened in Jesus' final days. Talk about the changes that took place. Explain why Jesus went through this painful death, to take the punishment for the things we have done wrong.

Countdown 3:
Keep those hands busy

The craft activities in this section are based on the theme of the cross. As you work, chat about the story from this session and what it means to you. Let the children ask you any questions they might have about Jesus' death on the cross.

☉1 Cross stained glass
15 minutes

What you need
- Glass paints and outliner (available from craft shops)
- Sheets of acetate suitable for glass painting (available from craft shops)

What you do
It might be good to do an example of this before the session so that you can show the group what to do. Demonstrate how to make the outline of a cross on the acetate, and then to create shapes around the outside. Show the children how to fill in the cross and shapes with different colours of glass paint. Give the materials to the group and help them create and paint their own cross designs. When they are dry, the acetates can be stuck to a window to let the light shine through!

As you work, chat about the story from this session and what it means to you. Let the children ask you questions as you work.

☉2 Cross picture poster
10 minutes

What you need
- Two pieces of card the same size, one black and one green
- Scissors
- Felt-tip pens or colouring pencils

What you do
Draw a hill shape outline on the green paper and the outline of three crosses on the hill. Cut along your outline. Stick the outline shape onto the black paper so that the crosses are in silhouette on the skyline.

On the bottom of the green paper the children write some words from the Bible passage such as 'They nailed Jesus to a cross' or 'Jesus shouted, "My God, my God, why have you deserted me?"' or just write 'Jesus died'. As you

World of a child
From the last session, children will have become aware that Jesus knew he was going to die. This story is shocking and, for children for whom the story is unfamiliar, it is especially shocking. However, tragic or violent deaths are unfortunately common in the media but be aware that children's knowledge and experience will vary enormously. This is an opportunity for you to share with the children how Jesus' death has changed your life and how he can forgive and change the lives of the children at **High Five**.

If a child wants to know more, do use the booklets *Friends with Jesus* or *Me+Jesus*, the two Scripture Union booklets that help children aged 5 to 7 and 8 to 10 find out what it means to follow Jesus. For more details see page 12 or visit www.scriptureunion.org.uk/shop

7

do this talk about what Jesus' death means to you and also how your life has been changed as a result.

 **Cross biscuits**
15 minutes

What you need
- 120 g (4 oz) butter
- 60 g (2 oz) caster sugar
- 180 g (6 oz) plain flour
- Baking utensils
- Oven

What you do
Be aware of health and safety, hygiene and allergy issues when making these biscuits. Preheat the oven to 190 °C/375 °F/Gas 5. Cream together the butter and sugar. (This is quite hard work, so let all the children take a short turn at this!) Add in the sifted flour and work the ingredients to get a smooth dough. Roll the dough out to about 1 cm thick and cut out cross-shaped biscuits. Put them on a greased baking sheet and bake for about 15 to 20 minutes.

Alternatively, if you don't have baking facilities where you meet, you could make these biscuits beforehand. Provide the group with different colours of icing and other cake decorations and encourage them to decorate the biscuits.

As you work, chat about the story from this session and what it means to you. Let the children ask you questions as you work.

Countdown 2:

Joining hands around the world

 *Countdown 2* **review**
10 minutes

What you need
- Resources from *Countdown 2* used in previous sessions: images of children, Fairtrade leaflets, posters of the UN Rights of the Child

What you do
Recap on the issues covered over the past six weeks – being the same but different, fair trade, children without choices, water. Look through some of the resources used during those sessions. Each child should share with a partner the things they have learnt about people

around the world; the things that have shocked or upset them; the things that have surprised them and the things they think they could do to make a difference to others. They may comment on how awful things are in the world. Explain that this is what happens when people live life without wanting to love and please God. This is the reason why Jesus had to die.

 *Change One Thing*
10 minutes

What you need
- *Change One Thing* sheets photocopied for each child (see www.scriptureunion.org.uk/highfive)
- Pens
- Large sheet of paper
- Marker pens

What you do
Introduce the *Change One Thing* sheet. What one thing could the children commit to changing? Make a list of possible changes on the large sheet of paper.

Ask the children to complete their own *Change One Thing* sheet to be used later in the *Countdown 1* prayer and praise section, then to be taken home.

 **What can we do?**
5 minutes

What you do
If this is relevant, remind the children of the fund-raising project you told them about in Session 5. Check how they are getting on and talk about what else you could do to bring about change.

Countdown 1:

Hands to praise and hands to pray

If you have sung together in previous sessions, continue to do so now. 'For God so loved the world' would be appropriate for this session. Otherwise, try one or two of these activities:

1 *Change One Thing* Prayers
5 minutes

What you need
- *Change One Thing* sheets from *Countdown 2*

What you do
Share the prayers written on the *Change One Thing* sheets. Ask the children to read out their prayers (but don't make them if they don't want to) or you could read out their prayers for them if they wish. You could even ask everyone to read out their prayers all at once, as a kind of prayer concert. This way, no one will feel self-conscious that people are listening to them – everyone will be praying at the same time!

2 Thank you for dying
10 minutes

What you need
- CD player
- *Sunday's Cool – Celebrate* CD by Mark and Helen Johnson, Out of the Ark Music, £14.50

What you do
Play or sing the song 'When I think about the cross' from the CD or using the lyrics on www.scriptureunion.org.uk/highfive as the children reflect on what they have learnt in this session about Jesus' death on the cross. You could print out the words so that the children can read them as they listen. End with a simple prayer thanking Jesus that he was willing to die on the cross to change us and the world.

8

Session 8
Strong hands

Mark 16:1–7
Jesus is alive!

Aim
To know that Jesus died on the cross for each one of us, but then rose from the dead. His hands are indeed strong hands.

Social justice theme
We will be reviewing all the **High Five** themes.

Jesus is alive – not only then but is alive today. This is the good news that he wants all people to know, that he is alive and wants us to get to know him better.

Countdown 5:

Hands up for fun and games

Choose one or more of these activities (depending on time) to introduce today's theme to your group. Jesus wants us to tell people everywhere about him, so that they can learn more about him too. We need to pass on the good news about Jesus. Talk about how we pass on messages which was what Jesus wanted his followers to do.

1 Chinese whispers
5 minutes

What you do
Sit the children in a circle. Whisper a short message to the child next to you and ask them to pass the message on to the person next to them. Continue around the circle until the last person repeats the message out loud. Repeat the game by asking different children to start with a new message.

Does the correct message always get passed round? What happens when people mishear the message?

2 Catch the ball
5 minutes

What you need
• Soft football or sponge ball

What you do
Ask the children to stand in a circle. The leader throws the football or sponge ball to someone else in the circle at random, who then passes the ball to someone else and so on. If the ball is dropped, that person has to sit out the next round. When they have missed a round, they can rejoin the game again. When you have

finished, talk briefly about how you have been passing something from one person to another.

3 Pass the squeeze
 *5 minutes*

What you do
The group should be seated in a circle on the floor, holding hands. Starting with one person, the child should squeeze the hand of the person next to them who then 'passes' the squeeze onto the person next to them and so on until the squeeze has been passed round the whole circle. Once the group has got the hang of this game, they can be timed to try to beat their time, passing the squeeze around the whole group in the quickest time possible.

Countdown 4:

Open the Bible

1 Story bag
5 minutes

What you need
• Bag containing a jar of spices, a large stone and a strip of white fabric
• Enlarged coded message "God has raised Jesus to life. He isn't here." and codecracker from page 55
• Codecracker

What you do
Recap on the events of Jesus' death from the previous week. Then read the story from Mark 16:1–7 bringing items out of the story bag at the relevant points in the story. After verse 3 as marked, ask the children what they think the women planned to do about the stone. (You may need to explain how the stone was huge

and acted as a door to keep people out and maybe keep the smell in!)

Continue the story. So what exactly did the man in a white robe say about Jesus?

After the children have given you some suggestions, show them this coded message of what the young man said and the codecracker. Ask the children to take it in turns to work out what the message is.

Explain that Jesus has been alive ever since! He is alive today and can be with us all the time.

Continue to explore the story using one or more of the suggestions below:

 **Reaction time**
5 minutes

What you need
- Bibles or photocopies of page 53
- Large sheets of paper with several thought bubbles
- Marker pens
- A prepared account by one leader of how they have responded to the news that Jesus is alive

What you do
Read the Bible passage together, with one child being the young man, and two reading the women's words. Then ask the children what they think would be the reaction of the other disciples when they heard the women's news. How do the children think *they* would have reacted to this news?

Share the ideas as a group and write them into the thought bubbles.

Explain to the children that Thomas wasn't with the disciples when the women told them the news, so he took some convincing; over a week in fact. Interview the leader who has prepared the account of their response. Ask some ordinary questions about good news and bad news they have received in the past, such as exam results, new job. Then ask them how they have responded to the good news that Jesus is alive.

 **News flash!**
20 minutes

What you need
- Video camera or tape recorder/MP3 player (optional)
- Bibles or photocopies of page 53

What you do
Read the Bible verses together. Working in pairs, one of the children plays the part of a news reporter and the other is Mary Magdalene. The reporter interviews Mary, focusing on her reaction to the empty tomb. What did she see? What did she hear? How did she feel?

These interviews can then be shared with the rest of the group. How would the children have felt in Mary's situation?

Countdown 3:
Keep those hands busy

The craft activities in this session remind the children of the good news that Jesus is alive!

As you work, share with the children how this fact makes a difference in your life.

 **Stone art**
20 minutes

What you need
- Large pebbles (clean!)
- Poster paints or paints mixed with PVA glue

What you do
Take a large pebble and decorate using poster paints or paint mixed with PVA glue. This pebble can be taken home, as a reminder that the stone was rolled away from the entrance of the tomb, and Jesus is alive. The designs could incorporate a cross or the name of Jesus.

If there is enough time and resources, the children could make more than one pebble as a gift for someone else.

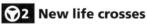 **New life crosses**
15 minutes

What you need
- Lolly sticks
- String or garden twine
- Beans eg runner beans, broad beans
- Plastic cups
- Soil
- Poster paint
- Collage materials
- Glue
- Marker pens

World of a child
Children know lots about magic in stories and may tend to see the resurrection as a magical act rather than the power of God to bring new life and conquer death with all its implications. Encourage them to ask questions out of curiosity and answer them as best you can. Of course, the important outcome of the resurrection is that Jesus is alive today. We want all children to know that Jesus can be with them in every place and at every time. Indeed he longs for them to enter into friendship with him.

Some children may have been bereaved recently. They may have been given all sorts of ideas about death and heaven and angels etc! That is no reason to soften the impact of the resurrection but is a call to be extra sensitive.

8

What you do

Make a cross out of two lolly sticks, bound together with string or twine. In a plastic cup, place some soil and a bean. Place the cross in the soil, so that as the bean grows, it entwines itself around the cross. This can remind the children that although people thought Jesus had died on the cross, he rose from the dead. Because of this we can have new life if we believe in him.

The cup could be decorated with paint or collage items, or with the words 'Jesus is alive' in marker pen.

Good news posters
20 minutes

What you need
- A4 paper
- Felt-tip pens

What you do

Mary Magdalene had good news to tell the disciples. Today there are many ways we can pass on good news – letter, telephone, email, and text message. Design a poster, telling the good news of Jesus Christ. The lettering could be in text language eg BTW JC died 4 U, or the poster could be designed and printed using a computer if one is available.

Display the finished posters around the room. Then ask the children to go round and see the good news that the posters display.

Countdown 2:

Joining hands around the world

Recap on the topics covered over the last seven weeks: same but different, Fairtrade, children without choices, water.

Fund-raising project
5 minutes

What you do

Continue to talk about how you are getting on with the project begun in Session 5. Give the children an outline of what has been happening and the amount you have raised so far. Let any children involved in the project tell the rest of the group what they have done towards the project.

 What next?
10 minutes

What you need
- Images from the *Countdown 2* themes in **High Five** plus images from newspapers of things that are wrong in the world – make sure these are suitable for the children in your group

What you do

Show the different images you have found. Talk about the many sad things there are in the world. Comment on the fact that this is not how God intended the world to be but, from the beginning, people have not lived the way he wanted. They have disobeyed him. And the result has been all these disasters. Jesus came to begin to put things right – to forgive us and to conquer death – and we too can bring about change with his help. Talk about how your fund-raising project is going to change things too.

Countdown 1:

Hands to praise and hands to pray

Finish your last session off by singing some of the songs you have learnt during the club. Make sure you include the children's favourite!

1 Good news Chinese whispers
10 minutes

What you need
- An object you have used in **High Five**, such as a cross or a medal or a salt dough model

What you do

Ask the children to sit in a circle and play Chinese whispers. Start with a message about what the good news of Jesus means to you. Once that has been passed round, encourage one of the group to start off a message about what they have learnt about Jesus over the past eight weeks. When everyone has had a go who wants to, conclude by thanking Jesus for who he is, what he has done for us, including the fun you have had at **High Five**.

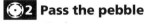 **Pass the pebble**

10 minutes

What you need

• The pebbles painted in *Countdown 3*

What you do

Sit in a circle and pass round a pebble from the *Countdown 3* activity. When a child is holding it, they can say something to God, either thanking him for something from **High Five** or asking him to do something in one of the world situations covered in *Countdown 2* over the last eight weeks. If a child does not want to do this, they can pass the object on to the next person.

Photocopiable Resources

Session 1

Mark 1:40–45

A man with leprosy came to Jesus and knelt down. He begged, "You have the power to make me well, if only you wanted to."

Jesus felt sorry for the man. So he put his hand on him and said, "I want to! Now you are well." At once the man's leprosy disappeared, and he was well.

After Jesus strictly warned the man, he sent him on his way. He said, "Don't tell anyone about this. Just go and show the priest that you are well. Then take a gift to the temple as Moses commanded, and everyone will know that you have been healed."

The man talked about it so much and told so many people, that Jesus could no longer go openly into a town. He had to stay away from the towns, but people still came to him from everywhere.

Session 2

Mark 7:31–37

Jesus left the region around Tyre and went by way of Sidon towards Lake Galilee. He went through the land near the ten cities known as Decapolis. Some people brought to him a man who was deaf and could hardly talk. They begged Jesus just to touch him.

After Jesus had taken him aside from the crowd, he stuck his fingers in the man's ears. Then he spat and put the spit on the man's tongue. Jesus looked up towards heaven, and with a groan he said, "Effatha!" which means "Open up!" At once the man could hear, and he had no more trouble talking clearly.

Jesus told the people not to say anything about what he had done. But the more he told them, the more they talked about it. They were completely amazed and said, "Everything he does is good! He even heals people who cannot hear or talk."

Session 3

Mark 8:1–10

One day another large crowd gathered around Jesus. They had not brought along anything to eat. So Jesus called his disciples together and said, "I feel sorry for these people. They have been with me for three days, and they don't have anything to eat. Some of them live a long way from here. If I send them away hungry, they might faint on their way home."

The disciples said, "This place is like a desert. Where can we find enough food to feed such a crowd?"

Jesus asked them how much food they had. They replied, "Seven small loaves of bread."

After Jesus told the crowd to sit down, he took the seven loaves and blessed them. He then broke the loaves and handed them to his disciples, who passed them out to the crowd. They also had a few little fish, and after Jesus had blessed these, he told the disciples to pass them around.

The crowd of about four thousand people ate all they wanted, and the leftovers filled seven large baskets.

As soon as Jesus had sent the people away, he got into the boat with the disciples and crossed to the territory near Dalmanutha.

Session 4

Mark 9:33–37

Jesus and his disciples went to his home in Capernaum. After they were inside the house, Jesus asked them, "What were you arguing about along the way?" They had been arguing about which one of them was the greatest, and so they did not answer.

After Jesus sat down and told the twelve disciples to gather around him, he said, "If you want the place of honour, you must become a slave and serve others!"

Then Jesus made a child stand near him. He put his arm around the child and said, "When you welcome even a child because of me, you welcome me. And when you welcome me, you welcome the one who sent me."

Session 5

Mark 10:17–31

As Jesus was walking down a road, a man ran up to him. He knelt down, and asked, "Good teacher, what can I do to have eternal life?"

Jesus replied, "Why do you call me good? Only God is good. You know the commandments. 'Do not murder. Be faithful in marriage. Do not steal. Do not tell lies about others. Do not cheat. Respect your father and mother.'"

The man answered, "Teacher, I have obeyed all these commandments since I was a young man."

Jesus looked closely at the man. He liked him and said, "There's one thing you still need to do. Go and sell everything you own. Give the money to the poor, and you will have riches in heaven. Then come with me." *

When the man heard Jesus say this, he went away gloomy and sad because he was very rich.

Jesus looked around and said to his disciples, "It's hard for rich people to get into God's kingdom!" The disciples were shocked to hear this. So Jesus told them again, "It's terribly hard to get into God's kingdom! In fact, it's easier for a camel to go through the eye of a needle than for a rich person to get into God's kingdom."

Jesus' disciples were even more amazed. They asked each other, "How can anyone ever be saved?"

Jesus looked at them and said, "There are some things that people cannot do, but God can do anything."

Peter replied, "Remember, we left everything to be your followers!"

Jesus told him:

"You can be sure that anyone who gives up home or brothers or sisters or mother or father or children or land for me and for the good news will be rewarded. In this world they will be given a hundred times as many houses and brothers and sisters and mothers and children and pieces of land, though they will also be ill-treated. And in the world to come, they will have eternal life. But many who are now first will be last, and many who are now last will be first."

Mark 12:41–44

Jesus was sitting in the temple near the offering box and watching people put in their gifts. He noticed that many rich people were giving a lot of money. Finally, a poor widow came up and put in two coins that were worth only a few pennies. Jesus told his disciples to gather around him. Then he said: I tell you that this poor widow has put in more than all the others. Everyone else gave what they didn't need. But she is very poor and gave everything she had. Now she doesn't have a penny to live on.

Session 6

Mark 10:32–45

The disciples were confused as Jesus led them towards Jerusalem, and his other followers were afraid. Once again, Jesus took the twelve disciples aside and told them what was going to happen to him. He said:

"We are now on our way to Jerusalem where the Son of Man will be handed over to the chief priests and the teachers of the Law of Moses. They will sentence him to death and hand him over to foreigners, who will make fun of him and spit on him. They will beat him and kill him. But three days later he will rise to life."

James and John, the sons of Zebedee, came up to Jesus and asked, "Teacher, will you do us a favour?"

Jesus asked them what they wanted, and they answered, "When you come into your glory, please let one of us sit at your right side and the other at your left."

Jesus told them, "You don't really know what you're asking! Are you able to drink from the cup that I must soon drink from or be baptized as I must be baptized?"

"Yes, we are!" James and John answered. Then Jesus replied, "You certainly will drink from the cup from which I must drink. And you will be baptized just as I must! But it isn't for me to say who will sit at my right side and at my left. That is for God to decide."

When the ten other disciples heard this, they were angry with James and John. But Jesus called the disciples together and said:

"You know that those foreigners who call themselves kings like to order their people around. And their great leaders have full power over the people they rule. But don't act like them. If you want to be great, you must be the servant of all the others. And if you want to be first, you must be everyone's slave. The Son of Man did not come to be a slave master, but a slave who will give his life to rescue many people."

Mark 12:28–34

One of the teachers of the Law of Moses came up while Jesus and the Sadducees were arguing. When he heard Jesus give a good answer, he asked him, "What is the most important commandment?"

Jesus answered, "The most important one says: 'People of Israel, you have only one Lord and God. You must love him with all your heart, soul, mind, and strength.' The second most important commandment says: 'Love others as much as you love yourself.' No other commandment is more important than these."

The man replied, "Teacher, you are certainly right to say there is only one God. It is also true that we must love God with all our heart, mind, and strength, and that we must love others as much as we love ourselves. These commandments are more important than all the sacrifices and offerings that we could possibly make."

When Jesus saw that the man had given a sensible answer, he told him, "You are not far from God's kingdom." After this, no one dared ask Jesus any more questions.

Session 7

Mark 14:43–52

Jesus was still speaking, when Judas the betrayer came up. He was one of the twelve disciples, and a mob of men armed with swords and clubs were with him. They had been sent by the chief priests, the nation's leaders, and the teachers of the Law of Moses. Judas had told them beforehand, "Arrest the man I greet with a kiss. Tie him up tight and lead him away."

Judas walked right up to Jesus and said, "Teacher!" Then Judas kissed him, and the men grabbed Jesus and arrested him.

Someone standing there pulled out a sword. He struck the servant of the high priest and cut off his ear.

Jesus said to the mob, "Why do you come with swords and clubs to arrest me like a criminal? Day after day I was with you and taught in the temple, and you didn't arrest me. But what the Scriptures say must come true."

All Jesus' disciples ran off and left him. One of them was a young man who was wearing only a linen cloth. And when the men grabbed him, he left the cloth behind and ran away naked.

Mark 15:24–28,33–37

They nailed Jesus to a cross and gambled to see who would get his clothes. It was about nine o'clock in the morning when they nailed him to the cross. On it was a sign that told why he was nailed there. It read, "This is the King of the Jews." The soldiers also nailed two criminals on crosses, one to the right of Jesus and the other to his left…

About midday the sky turned dark and stayed that way until around three o'clock. Then about that time Jesus shouted, "Eloi, Eloi, lema sabachthani?" which means, "My God, my God, why have you deserted me?"

Some of the people standing there heard Jesus and said, "He is calling for Elijah." One of them ran and grabbed a sponge. After he had soaked it in wine, he put it on a stick and held it up to Jesus. He said, "Let's wait and see if Elijah will come and take him down!" Jesus shouted and then died.

Session 8

Mark 16:1–7

After the Sabbath, Mary Magdalene, Salome, and Mary the mother of James bought some spices to put on Jesus' body. Very early on Sunday morning, just as the sun was coming up, they went to the tomb. On their way, they were asking one another, "Who will roll the stone away from the entrance for us?" *But when they looked, they saw that the stone had already been rolled away. And it was a huge stone!

The women went into the tomb, and on the right side they saw a young man in a white robe sitting there. They were alarmed.

The man said, "Don't be alarmed! You are looking for Jesus from Nazareth, who was nailed to a cross. God has raised him to life, and he isn't here. You can see the place where they put his body. Now go and tell his disciples, and especially Peter, that he will go ahead of you to Galilee. You will see him there, just as he told you."

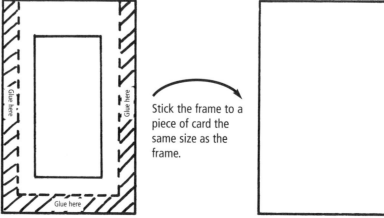

Stick the frame to a piece of card the same size as the frame.

Glue here

Glue here

Glue here

Bible Story Sum

Begin with the number of days these people were with Jesus? ....

Add on the number of people there. ....

Add on the number of times Jesus told the crowd to sit down ....

Divide by the number of loaves of bread Jesus took. ....

Take away the number of times Jesus blessed the food. ....

Divide by the number of Bible verses that tell this story. ....

Take away the number of times Jesus told the disciples that he cared for the people. ....

Divide by the number of this chapter in Mark's Gospel. ....

(You should be left with the number of baskets of food that were left over!) ....

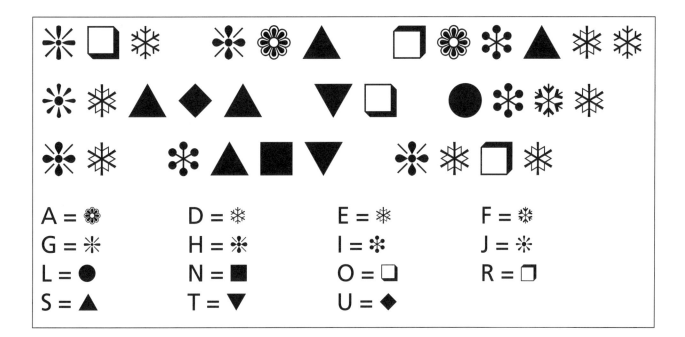

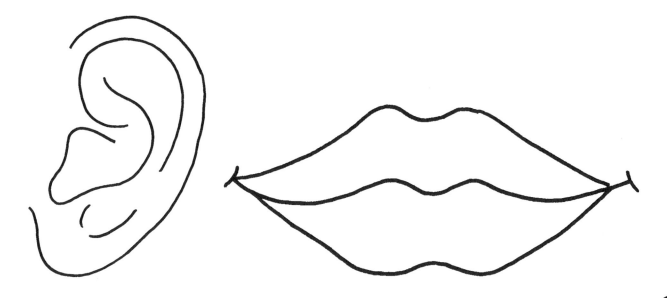

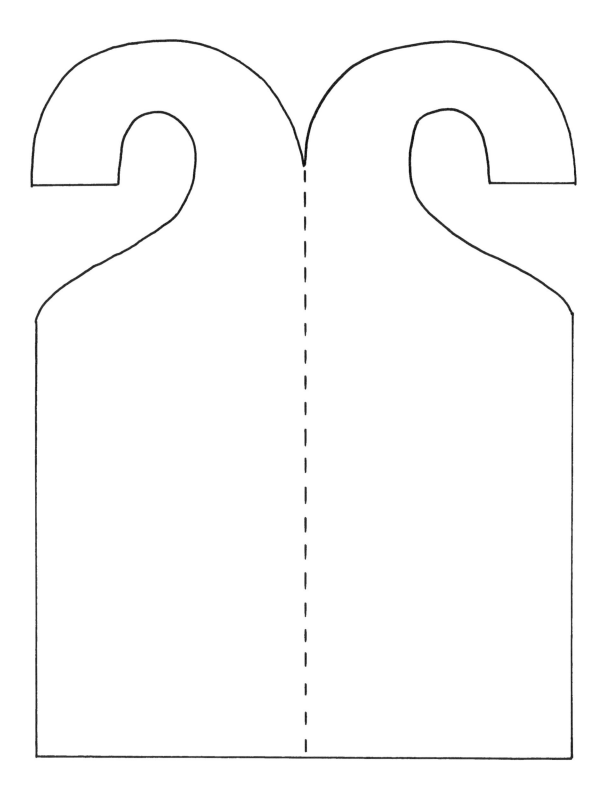

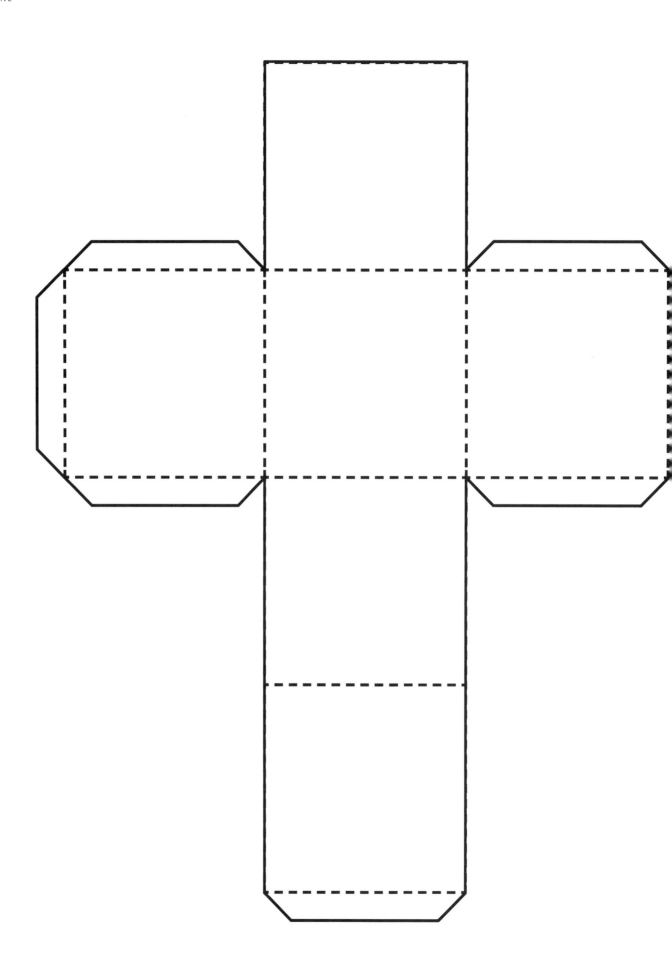

Declaration of the Rights of the Child

Proclaimed by the General Assembly of the United Nations in 1959

This is a simplified version, containing just an extract from some of the 10 principles.

Principle 3
The child shall be entitled from his birth to a name and a nationality.

Principle 5
The child who is physically, mentally or socially handicapped shall be given the special treatment, education and care required by his particular condition.

Principle 7
The child is entitled to receive education, which shall be free and compulsory, at least in the elementary stages.

Principle 8
The child shall in all circumstances be among the first to receive protection and relief.

Principle 9
The child shall be protected against all forms of neglect, cruelty and exploitation. He shall not be the subject of traffic, in any form.
The child shall not be admitted to employment before an appropriate minimum age.

Principle 10
The child shall be brought up in a spirit of understanding, tolerance, friendship among peoples.

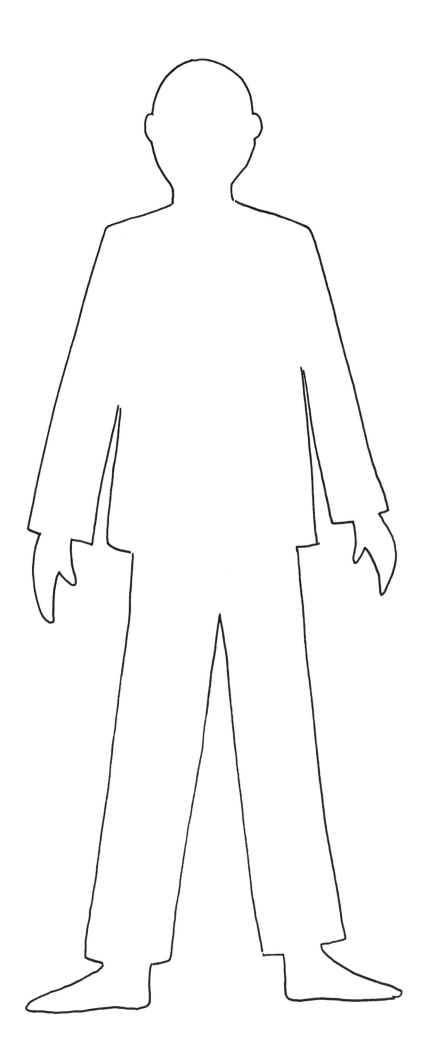

Other resources

Streetwise
Claire Derry and Julie Sharp

Streetwise is an eight-session midweek club programme that follows the accounts from Luke's Gospel of houses Jesus visited and people Jesus met. It includes games, prayers, stories and discussion. The Streetwise DVD can also be used as part of the programme.
£8.99 978 1 85999 767 3

Awesome!
Sue Clutterham

Together with the *Awesome!* DVD, *Awesome!* helps children explore who Jesus is using signs from John's Gospel. *Awesome!* is a flexible programme aimed at midweek groups looking to attract non-churched children aged 7 to 11. It has plenty of introductory ideas, ways of presenting the Bible and suggestions for follow-up.
£9.99 978 1 84427 153 5

Rocky Road
Rosey King

A ten-session programme for leaders running a midweek club for children, based on the story of Moses. *Rocky Road* includes gripping storytelling ideas, imaginative crafts and relationship-building opportunities. Can be used as a follow-up programme to a *Pyramid Rock* holiday club.
£9.99 978 1 84427 183 2

Clues2Use

Jean Elliott

Join the Landlubbers pirates as they follow clues to discover Jesus in the 21st century! Using the *Jesus Quest* DVD, this eight-session midweek club programme helps children see how Jesus is always with them. Can be used as a follow-up programme to a *Landlubbers* holiday club.

£9.99 978 1 84427 113 9

So, Why God?

Steve Hutchinson

How do you introduce children to the Christian faith? Their questions are a good starting point! *So, Why God?* seeks to answer questions children ask about the Christian faith using the Bible and the stories of group leaders themselves.

A 12-week discipleship course for children aged 7 to 11.

£9.99 978 1 84427 222 8

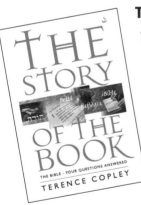

The Story of the Book

Terence Copley

Written in an easy-to-understand style, The Story of the Book encourages readers to ask and find out the answers to all the questions they have about the Bible, its past, present and future.

The book is aimed at anyone who uses the Bible in their ministry and who wants to know more about God's Word.

£8.99 978 1 84427 131 5

eye level clubs...

- are for boys and girls aged 5 to 11.
- are for children who are not yet part of a church (as well as those who are).
- don't assume that children know much about Jesus or have had any experience of church.
- recognise that all children are open to God and the wonder of his world, and that all children can have valid spiritual experiences, regardless of church background.
- aim to give children one of the best hours in their week.
- provide opportunities for appropriate and respectful relationships between children and adults, working in small groups.
- plan to introduce children to the Bible in ways that allow for imagination, exploration and learning difficulties.
- are led by those who long to see children become lifelong followers of Jesus Christ.
- are led by those who will put themselves at a child's level, so that together they can catch sight of Jesus.